One Crack Out

DATE DUE

One Crack Out

Revised edition

David French

TALONBOOKS
2003

Talonbooks
P.O. Box 2076, Vancouver, British Columbia, Canada V6B 3S3
www.talonbooks.com

Typeset in New Baskerville and printed and bound in Canada.

First Printing: November 2003

National Library of Canada Cataloguing in Publication Data
French, David, 1939–
    One crack out / David French.

    A play.
    ISBN 0-88922-488-9

    I. Title.
PS8561.R44O5 2003   C812'.54   C2003-910970-4

The publisher gratefully acknowledges the financial support of the
Canada Council for the Arts; the Government of Canada through the
Book Publishing Industry Development Program; and the Province of
British Columbia through the British Columbia Arts Council for our
publishing activities.

 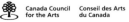

For Bill Glassco

One Crack Out was first produced by the Tarragon Theatre, Toronto, on May 24, 1975, with the following cast:

CHARLIE EVANS . . . . Les Carlson
HELEN . . . . Brenda Donohue
SUITCASE SAM. . . . . Al Kozlik
BULLDOG . . . . Robert O'Ree
JACK THE HAT . . . . Richard Donat
AL . . . . Allan Aarons
EARL. . . . . Larry Reynolds
WANDA. . . . . Wendy Thatcher
MCKEE. . . . . Thomas Hauff
GREG . . . . George R. Robertson
Directed by Bill Glassco
Designed by Eoin Sprott
Costumes by Rosalyn Mina
Lighting by John Stammers

One Crack Out was presented at the Phoenix Theatre, New York, NY, in January, 1978, with the following cast:

CHARLIE EVANS . . . . Kenneth Welsh
HELEN . . . . Teri Garr
SUITCASE SAM . . . . James Greene
BULLDOG . . . . Al Freeman, Jr.
JACK THE HAT . . . . Norman Snow
AL . . . . Jerry Zaks
EARL . . . . Ed Cambridge
WANDA . . . . Christine Baranski
MCKEE . . . . John Aquino
Directed by Daniel Freudenberger
Designed by James Tilton
Costumes by Julie Weiss
Lighting by Paul H. Everett

Characters

Charlie Evans
Helen
Suitcase Sam
Bulldog
Jack the Hat
Al
Earl
Wanda
McKee
Greg

Place

Earl's pool room and Charlie's apartment.

Time

Two days in November, 1975.

ACT ONE

Scene One

The lights come up on the pool hall. It is an old seedy place in need of a good coat of paint. This particular type of poolhall is among the last of its kind. Even the saloon-like swinging doors are a holdover from the past.

In the background is a counter with stools. On the counter: a radio, cash register, and a coffee percolator. Behind the counter is a telephone which regular customers are allowed to use. Stage left of the counter is a Coke machine. Against the wall stage right is a small bench and a pinball machine. Also along this wall: a door reading simply "Washroom", the blackboard for keeping score, and the cue racks.

The downstage wall of the washroom is missing so that the audience views its interior: a urinal, a toilet, a sink, paper towel dispenser, a rusty oil drum for the used towels, a wall mirror, and a radiator. Some graffiti. Above the urinal is an opaque window. Just inside the door is a light switch. Until the washroom is actually used for specific scenes, it is kept dark.

Upstage, the swinging doors lead into the poolhall proper from an offstage vestibule. A front door (unseen) is also offstage.

Dominating the room, in the foreground, is a pool table. Over it hangs a light with a shade.

It is around noon on a November day, 1975.

JACK THE HAT and AL, a cabdriver, are shooting pool. The HAT is in his late twenties, thin and pale. He wears a grey pinstripe suit, striped shirt with a black tie, black shoes, and a wide-brimmed grey fedora with a black band—his trademark. EARL, the owner of the pool hall, is behind the counter, reading the Racing Form. He is a rugged man in his mid-fifties, with a paralyzed right hand.

JACK THE HAT: (*chalking up*) Who do you like, Earl?

EARL: I dunno … Orange Willie in the first.

JACK THE HAT: She'll be the favourite. You don't stab a big winner betting even. I'll go with Spinning Wheel.

AL: The Hat likes the long shots, don't you, Hat?

EARL: Jack, you can afford to get burnt. At closing time I count myself lucky to break even.

Enter BULLDOG. He is around forty, well-built and expensively dressed. He carries his pool cue in a black carrying case.

AL: (*to EARL*) Look who's back.

BULLDOG: (*shaking hands*) Hey, there, Jack. How's it going?

JACK THE HAT: Okay, man. Hear you been outa town.

BULLDOG: (*hangs up his coat*) The weasel I was hunting went on the lam.

JACK THE HAT: Yeah?

BULLDOG: Took me three weeks to smoke him out. The man paid for it, though. I put him in a wheelchair.

AL: Saul Snider, the bookie.

BULLDOG: And when he's able to walk and don't pay his debt, I'll break his legs again. (*He sits at the counter*) So, Al, how's with you? Still practicing your stroke?

AL: (*touches his crotch*) Stroke this.

BULLDOG: I'd need a magnifying glass, Al. Bet even you have trouble finding it.

AL: You're so full of it, man. When I was a kid, I slid down a slide and cut myself there. It took thirteen stitches. One stitch for every inch.

BULLDOG: One and three make four, Al.

AL: I still got the scar to prove it.

BULLDOG: Bet that's all he's got, Earl, a scar.

AL: Very funny.

> *Enter WANDA, a hooker in her mid-twenties. She carries a tote bag over her shoulder.*

BULLDOG: Don't look now, Earl, but I think the sewer just backed up. (*Takes his cue from its case and screws it together*)

WANDA: Then shut your mouth and it won't overflow. Hiya, Jack.

BULLDOG: (*to EARL*) Keep letting hookers in here, you'll have the Pussy Posse sniffing around.

AL: You never complained when you pimped for her.

BULLDOG: Who asked you?

WANDA: He even dresses better now he's a collector. Look at him. Three-hundred dollar suits.

JACK THE HAT: You wanta talk, Wanda, talk on the street.

WANDA: Sorry, Hat. (*She sits on the bench, biding her time*)

> *Pause.*

AL: (*chalking up*) Know what I heard, Jack?

JACK THE HAT: What?

AL: I heard there's a man in Kansas can wear out two chalks before a guy gets off his first shot.

BULLDOG: That's a crock.

13

AL: That's what I heard.

JACK THE HAT: Who told you that?

BULLDOG: Some mental patient.

AL: I heard it from a guy in my cab. He just come back from there. He oughta know.

JACK THE HAT: (*to BULLDOG*) Maybe he's right.

BULLDOG: Any man says his dick is longer than his shoe size can't be trusted. Why do you play him, Jack? The man's a joke.

AL: Up yours, Bulldog. I never said I believed him, did I? I said I heard.

BULLDOG: (*grabs a chalk*) Know how long it takes to wear out *one* chalk? And you say this guy uses up *two* before the other guy gets off a shot? Don't insult my intelligence ... Gimme a coffee, Earl. No sugar.

WANDA: (*seizing the moment*) Hat, can I talk to you? It's strictly business.

JACK THE HAT: What do you want?

WANDA: Can you save a life? I'm gasping.

JACK THE HAT: Gimme a minute, Al. I'll be right back. (*To WANDA*) C'mon. (*He sets down his cue and heads for the washroom, WANDA following*)

AL: Throw me a cloth, Earl. (*He takes a rag from EARL and runs it along the edge of the table, then sits on the bench*)

BULLDOG: Hey, Al, you're not sore, are you? I was just ribbing you ... (*To EARL*) The man's touchy.

> *JACK THE HAT and WANDA enter the washroom. JACK switches on the light and closes the door.*

JACK THE HAT: Where the hell you been? You owe me three hundred. Let's have it.

WANDA: Jack, I've been sick. Didn't you hear? That's why I never come around.

JACK THE HAT: Don't story me.

WANDA: It's true. I had my appendix out. Haven't been able to work. And the few bucks I had in the bank, I blew on hospital bills. See for yourself. (*She shows him her scar*) I didn't get that from a john with a chipped tooth.

JACK THE HAT: All right. What do you want?

WANDA: Thanks, Hat. I'd like some coke. A spoon.

JACK THE HAT: Let's see the half a yard.

WANDA: Jack, I was hoping you'd carry me a while longer. I start back to work tonight. See, I've got this john coming in. I get seven bills for two days.

JACK THE HAT: So who's the coke for?

WANDA: The last time he was here, he said he wanted to try it. I wanta keep him happy.

JACK THE HAT: All right, but don't make me wait again, understand? (*He reaches under the sink, rips off a small piece of tinfoil taped to the bottom, and hands it to her*) I want the three and a half by Wednesday night.

WANDA: Okay, Hat, thanks … (*As JACK reaches for the door*) Jack?

JACK THE HAT: What?

WANDA: Can I bite you for another fifty and make it an even four?

JACK THE HAT: Don't press your luck, Wanda. See the sharks if you need fifty.

WANDA: The sharks? No, thanks.

JACK THE HAT: Hustle your tail, why don't you? There's a roomful of men out there.

JACK THE HAT exits the washroom and returns to the table. The game resumes … WANDA unfolds the tinfoil to reveal a small amount of cocaine. She sits on the toilet, rummages through her tote bag, and brings out a paper matchbox. Using the folded corner, she scoops up some powder and snorts it.

BULLDOG: (*as JACK returns to the table*) So, Jack, how's the action been? Much happening?

JACK THE HAT: I played Charlie Evans three days in a row. He's going bad.

BULLDOG: No shit?

EARL: Never seen him lose control like that.

AL: He'll get it back, Charlie.

JACK THE HAT: We played three sessions, four games a session, and I cracked him out.

BULLDOG: How much you take him for?

JACK THE HAT: Twelve hundred.

EARL: Hundred a game.

BULLDOG: Twelve hundred? I'm impressed.

JACK THE HAT: Broke his cue in half he was so pissed off.

AL: What'd you expect, Hat? You tapped him. He don't have a dime to put in a meter.

BULLDOG: Only a two-dollar player blows his cool.

AL: Listen to who's talking. I seen you throw a cue ball at some guy once. All because his shoes squeaked.

BULLDOG: The hell you did.

AL: When you're losing, if a guy coughs or scratches himself, you go ape-shit.

BULLDOG: That's different … Anyway, we all know why Evans won't play me. It's no secret.

AL: That ain't the reason, Bulldog. He just don't play collectors ... It's not personal.

BULLDOG: Everything's personal. The man thinks he's too good to play me, yet he plays every punk or low-life who sticks his nose in the door.

AL: Is that why you went after his wife? Man, I'd ice you if you ever did that to me.

BULLDOG: (*suddenly dangerous*) Shut your mouth, you. Talk to me like that and I'll rip your tongue out.

> *The room falls silent.*

EARL: Relax, Bulldog. Al don't mean nothing, do you, Al?

BULLDOG: (*laughs*) Did you hear that, Jack? He'd ice me. (*To AL*) How would you do that, cabdriver? Stick me with your thirteen-inch ice-pick?

> *Enter CHARLIE EVANS. He wears a black leather coat, blue jeans, and sneakers. He is forty-two.*

BULLDOG: Looks like a live one just walked in. What'd you think, Jack? Should I fire on him?

CHARLIE: (*crossing to get a Coke from the machine*) Know something, Bulldog? If you could shoot pool the way you shoot off your mouth, you might be Champ.

BULLDOG: I'm ready anytime you are, Evans. Pick up a cue.

CHARLIE: (*ignoring BULLDOG*) Sam hasn't been in today, has he, Earl?

EARL: Not yet, Charlie.

AL: Probably take him a while to get from the airport.

CHARLIE: How's it going, Al?

AL: Not so good. I'm down two.

BULLDOG: (*to CHARLIE*) The Hat tells me you played him twelve games. Play me and I'll spot you points.

CHARLIE: Don't you ever give up?

AL: He don't have his cue with him, do you, Charlie?

BULLDOG: He can have mine. I'll get another.

EARL: You heard him, Bulldog. He don't wanta play. Leave him alone.

BULLDOG: (*to EARL*) Look, I haven't played all month. That gives him the edge ... (*To CHARLIE*) You want thirty points? I'll give you thirty.

CHARLIE: I told you six months ago, and I meant it. I don't play collectors.

BULLDOG: The man has principles.

CHARLIE: That's right, I got principles.

BULLDOG: Too bad your wife don't feel the same. I guess it just don't run in the family.

CHARLIE: You sonofabitch! (*He springs at BULLDOG, who sidesteps him and smashes him to the floor*)

EARL: (*rushing in to break it up*) Stop it, goddammit. Hit him once more, Bulldog, and you're barred. I don't want heat in here.

BULLDOG: The man jumped me. I was just defending myself.

CHARLIE: (*gets to his feet, his mouth bleeding*) Think a little blood will get me to play, Bulldog? Well, think again.

BULLDOG: Never say no, hustler. Life has a way of making us eat our words.

AL: (*crosses to CHARLIE*) You okay, Charlie? You hurt?

CHARLIE: I'm okay. Leave me alone. I'm fine. (*He enters the washroom, takes a paper towel, and administers to his mouth*)

EARL: (*to* BULLDOG) I run a quiet room here, understand? I wanta keep it that way.

WANDA: What happened, Charlie? Somebody hit you?

CHARLIE: Bulldog.

WANDA: That psycho. One of these days someone's gonna take him down. I just hope I live to see it. (*She exits the washroom—To* BULLDOG) Why don't you pick on someone your own size for a change?

BULLDOG: Why don't you go stand on the corner? Maybe some wino will make you an offer.

WANDA: You're behind the times, Bulldog. I don't walk the street looking for tricks. I have my own set-up at home. (*She moves to the pinball machine and begins to play*)

> *The phone rings behind the counter.* EARL *answers it.*

EARL: Hello … Just a minute. (*To* JACK THE HAT) For you, Jack. You wanta take it?

JACK THE HAT: Yeah, sure. (*He carries his cue behind the counter and takes the receiver*) Yeah? … Okay, I'll be there in five. (*He hangs up and unscrews his cue*)

AL: Hey, what gives …

JACK THE HAT: (*putting the cue in its case*) Later, man. I gotta split. It's business. (*He hands the case to* EARL *who puts it under the counter*)

AL: (*gestures at the scoreboard*) Well, I got the points.

JACK THE HAT: (*crosses to the corner pocket and retrieves his money*) Can't be helped. Next time we'll just start over. (*He puts the money in his wallet and slips on his overcoat*)

BULLDOG: Looks like it's just us, Al. Rack up the balls.

AL: (*returns his cue to the rack*) I'm driving cab.

BULLDOG: Don't be stupid. You just lost a hundred. You wanta win it back or not?

AL: (*retrieving his money from the pocket*) For the record, Bulldog. Guys crap in my cab, right? They vomit, they mainline, they get out and run. Still, I don't break legs to pay the rent, and I don't take money off guys that do.

JACK THE HAT: It's just a job, Al.

BULLDOG: He's just parroting Evans. (*He takes a large roll of bills from his pocket*) Don't be a jerk, Al. There's enough here to buy your own cab. Now you wanta play or don't you?

AL: Will you give me thirty points?

BULLDOG: (*racking up the balls*) What do you take me for, a mark? I'm the one oughta get points.

JACK THE HAT: (*to AL*) He's been away from the game a month, remember? ... (*As CHARLIE exits the washroom*) Any you guys going to the races? Al?

AL: Naw, I think I'll stay here and clean out Bulldog. (*He helps rack up the balls*) I always wanted my own cab.

BULLDOG: Dream on. The only thing you'll clean out today are your pockets. (*He flips a dime on the table*) Call it.

AL: Heads.

BULLDOG: Tails. I break. (*He puts cotton batting in his ears, then breaks*)

JACK THE HAT: What about you, Charlie? There's a daily double I wanta bet. I can't make it to the track.

CHARLIE: Sure. I'll run it out for you ... I'm gonna give Sam a few more minutes. Case he got stuck in traffic. (*He sits at the counter*)

JACK THE HAT: I wanta put fifty dollars on these two horses. (*He writes the names on a piece of paper*) Here. (*He hands CHARLIE the paper and a fifty-dollar bill*) The nags come in, I'll remember you. (*He crosses to the front door*) Anyone calls, Earl, I'll be back around five. (*He exits*)

> WANDA *moves to the counter and switches on the radio. ... BULLDOG switches it off.*

WANDA: (*to EARL*) Say, Earl, you're not married anymore, are you? ... You must get lonely, sleeping all alone.

EARL: Actually, I prefer it.

WANDA: Do you have a woman in your life?

EARL: No, and I can't afford you, either.

WANDA: I'm cheap at fifty bucks.

CHARLIE: Thought you had your own business at home, Wanda?

WANDA: I do. I've got a sweet deal now, Charlie. Found myself a sugar daddy.

BULLDOG: Then what the hell you hustling Earl for?

WANDA: 'Cause I'm broke, that's why. He's flying in tonight for two days and I'm short. (*To CHARLIE*) I wanta buy liquor and stuff, you know? I wanta make a good impression.

CHARLIE: Can't you phone another trick?

WANDA: No, I threw away my book. The deal is I gotta be there when he comes in or it's no deal. Hell, it's worth it. I make seven bills for two days. Not bad, huh?

EARL: I'm in the wrong business.

WANDA: I searched his pockets the first time. He had close to four grand. If I play my cards right, I'll get him up to a thousand. The only thing is I gotta keep it fresh. Last month I hadda hire another girl. He wanted a threesome.

CHARLIE: How was it?

WANDA: Terrific … Say, Charlie, what're you doing this afternoon? Wanta kill some time?

CHARLIE: The price is too high.

WANDA: What? Half a yard?

CHARLIE: I'm flat broke.

SAM: (*off*) ALL RIGHT, YOU ROUNDERS, UP AGAINST THE WALL, THIS IS A BUST!

Enter SUITCASE SAM.

CHARLIE: Welcome back, Sam. What took you so long?

WANDA: Jeez, I almost swallowed my stash. I thought it was the narcs.

SAM: You've swallowed more than that, Wanda. A little dope wouldn't hurt. Hey, Earl. (*He shakes EARL's hand*)

EARL: Glad you're back, Suitcase … Where's your tan?

SAM: What tan? You know me, I wear socks on the beach … (*To CHARLIE*) Like the new coat? Bought it off a booster in Miami.

CHARLIE: Pretty sharp.

SAM: (*looks around*) Some things never change. A week ago I left here, the same guys were standing around … Have a cigar, Earl. Boosted it myself at the airport.

EARL: Expensive.

CHARLIE: So how was the honeymoon?

SAM: Don't ask. Why people shell out good bucks to go to Florida is beyond me. The hotels here are better. (*To AL*) Catch. (*He tosses AL a cigar*)

CHARLIE: I'm glad you're back, Sam. I really need to get back to work.

SAM: Jesus, let me catch my breath, will you? I just stepped off the plane ... What's new with you, Wanda?

WANDA: I had my appendix out.

SAM: No guff?

WANDA: I'll show you at my place for half a bill.

SAM: Sorry, doll. I'm a married man.

BULLDOG: (*to SAM*) What? You don't say hello anymore, Suitcase? You can't spare a cigar?

SAM: You don't smoke, Bulldog.

BULLDOG: Al don't smoke, either.

AL: Maybe I'll learn.

> *CHARLIE takes SAM aside.*

CHARLIE: Listen, we need to talk, Sam. It's important.

SAM: Why? What's wrong?

CHARLIE: Not here. In private.

SAM: Okay. Sure.

> *CHARLIE and SAM head for the washroom. WANDA returns to the pinball machine.*

BULLDOG: (*to EARL*) What the hell is this, Union Station?

> *CHARLIE and SAM enter the washroom ... CHARLIE checks himself out in the mirror.*

SAM: What's on your mind?

CHARLIE: (*beat*) I'm busted, Sam. I lost a bundle while you were gone. Twelve hundred.

SAM: Twelve hundred? How'd you do that?

CHARLIE: I played the Hat twelve games, and he beat me.

SAM: All twelve?

CHARLIE: I'm going bad, Sam ... I need to get out on the road. Maybe that'll break the lock I'm in.

SAM: What is it, Charlie? The thing with Helen?

CHARLIE: It's like I'm cracking up. I always figured I was in the driver's seat, and now ... Ever look in the mirror and wonder who that is looking back?

SAM: Usually it's me shaving.

CHARLIE: I'm forty-two, Sam. For the first time in my life it's like I'm losing my grip ... The other day I almost ...

SAM: What?

CHARLIE: I'm ashamed to tell you.

SAM: What, Charlie?

CHARLIE: I was driving down the Don Valley, and I ... I almost swung the car into the bridge.

SAM: What? On purpose?

CHARLIE: Stupid, huh?

SAM: You ever do that, Charlie, and I swear I'll piss on your grave once a week for the rest of my life.

CHARLIE: You would, too.

SAM: You can make book on it ... Look, Charlie, most guys go through this one time or another. It's not a big deal.

CHARLIE: Easy for you to say, Sam.

SAM: It's all in your attitude ... Besides, you've been stressed-out lately, what with Helen's little fling with Bulldog ... Maybe you should try getting it on with someone else.

CHARLIE: All right. Maybe I will. Maybe in Quebec.

SAM: Quebec? ...

24

CHARLIE: Yeah. I figured tomorrow we'd drive up to Ottawa and work our way to Montreal.

SAM: Charlie, Charlie.

CHARLIE: What?

SAM: I can't do it, Charlie. I don't have the flash money. Miami cost me a fortune, and I got careless at the hotel. I got conned into a crap game with a bunch of high rollers ...

CHARLIE: You lost the front money?

SAM: Most of it. And you know we can't work our hustle without a suitcase fulla dough. The mark's gotta see real dough.

CHARLIE: (*beat*) I smell a story, Sam. I knew something was wrong when you walked in today ... What's happened? You find another partner?

SAM: It ain't that.

CHARLIE: No? C'mon. Give it to me straight.

SAM: All right, Charlie ... I'm quitting. I'm packing it in.

CHARLIE: Quitting? ...

SAM: I'm too old for this. I wanta get out before it's too late.

CHARLIE: Whose idea is it? Yours or Candy's?

SAM: It's mine. She had nothing to do with it.

CHARLIE: I'll bet.

SAM: Think this is easy, Charlie? I'm trying to tell you how it is ... Her father's old. No one to take care of him. So Candy and me, we figured we'd go down east ...

CHARLIE: What's in it for you, Sam? You've always got an angle. Let's have it.

SAM: He owns a motel just outside Moncton. He's too sick to run it ... It'll be ours when the old guy croaks.

CHARLIE: Which oughta be any day.

SAM: It's a big motel, Charlie. Twenty units. Swimming pool. Tennis court. A guy can make a buck in the summers, spend the winters down south ...

CHARLIE: And what about me, Sam? We're partners, remember? A man's not supposed to shaft his partner.

SAM: Who's shafting you? ... Can't you find another partner? What about Al?

CHARLIE: Get the hell outa here, Sam, before I lose my temper!

SAM: Charlie, be reasonable ...

CHARLIE: I said get lost. I don't need you, man ... I don't need anyone.

SAM: Okay, my friend, if that's the way you want it ... (*He crosses to the door*) I was hoping you'd understand.

CHARLIE: What's to understand? You lost your nerve.

SAM: It don't take much, Charlie. Just a little arithmetic. Think I wanta turn fifty and still be hustling pool? Watching every time a mark walks in the door? Living in crummy hotel rooms in two-bit towns? That's for punks. And every year it gets harder 'cause you start to get known. Pretty soon you got no towns to play in, and you're over the hill. What happens then, Charlie?

CHARLIE: It's all I know ...

SAM: Well, I got a chance to get out, and I'm taking it ... I'll see you around. (*He exits the washroom*)

CHARLIE: (*to himself*) Yeah, sure ...

SAM: Be good, Earl. Catch you later.

EARL: Right, Sam. Take care.

AL: Ciao.

> *SAM exits … After a moment, CHARLIE exits the washroom.*

WANDA: (*at the pinball machine*) What a lotta deadbeats, Earl. No one can help a girl out … What do you say, Charlie? You've got fifty bucks in your pocket.

CHARLIE: It's not mine. It don't belong to me.

WANDA: You don't know what you're missing, hon.

CHARLIE: Believe me, Wanda, I'm tempted. It's just that I gotta get to the track.

WANDA: Jeez, I may never win Miss America, but not many guys turn me down for a horse.

CHARLIE: Two horses.

WANDA: Will you give me a lift home at least? It's on the way.

CHARLIE: Okay, kid, but I'm in a hurry. Let's go.

WANDA: (*to EARL*) One-track mind, this guy.

> *Blackout.*

Scene Two

CHARLIE's flat.

All we see of it is the bed-sitting room and the hallway. A coffee table in front of a sofa. An armchair, a few prints on the walls. A TV and hi-fi set.

HELEN lounges on the sofa, doing a crossword puzzle in a newspaper. She is a slim and attractive woman in her late twenties.

CHARLIE enters, throws his coat on the armchair ... He and HELEN glance at each other ... CHARLIE goes offstage and returns with a bottle of beer.

CHARLIE: Don't you have to work?

HELEN: My night off ... Where you been?

CHARLIE: Down at the poolhall ... (*Pause*) I didn't hear you come in last night. It musta been late.

HELEN: (*into her crossword*) I had to fill in for one of the girls.

CHARLIE: Why didn't you wake me?

HELEN: You were sound asleep.

CHARLIE: You always used to wake me.

HELEN: (*puts down the newspaper*) Look, I don't wanta fight, Charlie ... I had a hard night. Some guy sat in the front row with his hat in his lap from six o'clock on.

Pause.

CHARLIE: I saw Bulldog today. He was down at Earl's ... You knew he was back in town, didn't you?

HELEN: I already told you, Charlie. I don't wanta fight.

CHARLIE: Didn't you?

28

HELEN: (*beat*) All right, so he came by the club last night. Is that what you want to hear?

CHARLIE: And you filled in for one of the girls, huh? Christ.

HELEN: I can't help it if he dropped by the club, can I? Is that my fault? ... Anyway, all we did was go for a drink.

CHARLIE: A drink?

HELEN: He wanted to go to his place but I told him no. I told him the same thing I told him before he left last month: it's over, finished.

CHARLIE: And what'd he say?

HELEN: It's not something I care to repeat.

CHARLIE: Did you wanta go to his place?

HELEN: What's that gotta do with anything? The fact is, I didn't, so let's drop it ... Charlie, I know how it's affected you, all this, and I'm sorry, I am. What'll it take to make you believe that?

CHARLIE: Doesn't matter what I believe, does it?

HELEN: I wish I'd never opened my mouth. I wish to Christ I'd never. I shoulda known better.

CHARLIE: The day you told me ... I almost bought a piece. I wanted to kill that scumbag.

HELEN: Just don't do anything stupid, now that he's back. Promise me, Charlie ... It's not like he twisted my arm.

CHARLIE: You don't have to remind me.

HELEN: All I'm saying is I'm just as much to blame as he is ...

CHARLIE: I still can't get it outa my head, you and him together ... all the time I was on the road. Couldn't get enough, could you?

29

HELEN: You hadn't touched me in months, Charlie. My God, what do you think all the fights were about?

CHARLIE: But why that cockroach? Why him of all people?

HELEN: You know damn well I didn't know who he was … He just showed up at the club the night you and Sam went to Sudbury. Offered to buy me a drink. He was very charming.

CHARLIE: Then why'd you refuse?

HELEN: You think he's the first guy I've shot down, Charlie? Don't kid yourself.

CHARLIE: You didn't refuse the second night, though, did you?

HELEN: Do we have to go through all this again? What's the point! It just eats away at you.

CHARLIE: I wanta understand, that's all. I wanta understand how you could let that—

HELEN: (*cutting in*) Then will you let me finish and not blow up? … This is the last time, Charlie. The last time I wanta discuss it …

CHARLIE: All right.

HELEN: (*beat*) That first night he asked me out, I said no. That's all there was to it. Sure, he turned me on. I couldn't help that, could I? It's not something you switch on and off … (*She lights a cigarette*)

CHARLIE: Go on.

HELEN: Anyway, that night I came home and went to bed … and I thought about him.

CHARLIE: Romeo with a heart of ice.

HELEN: The next night he was back at the club. In the middle of my act I looked down and there he was in the front row … When I left that night, he was waiting on the steps...I was hoping he wouldn't be there, because I'd already decided if he was, I'd go with him.

CHARLIE: Just like that?

HELEN: I thought it'd be simple, Charlie ... All right, maybe I'm naïve, but that's what I thought. I figured, Why not? I'll never see this guy again. Just a one-night stand.

CHARLIE: Old Charlie will never know.

HELEN: Don't get self-righteous, okay? I know damn well what you and Sam are like on the road ... The way I figured it, if I lived out one of my fantasies, it might even help us in bed.

CHARLIE: And you thought you were using *him*? What a laugh. Don't you understand, Helen? He only hit on you for one reason and one reason only: you're my wife!

Offstage, we hear a door open and close.

SAM: (*off*) Anybody home?

HELEN: It's Sam.

SAM: (*off*) Charlie? You home?

CHARLIE: In here.

Enter SAM. HELEN hugs him.

HELEN: You're looking good ... Candy phoned. Said you had a great time in Miami.

SAM: Even wore a pair of flip-flops. A first ... Something tells me she's ruined my image.

HELEN: You're terrible, Sam. Why can't you just admit you're nuts about her?

SAM: What? And spoil a good marriage?

31

CHARLIE: (*to HELEN*) Did Candy tell you they're moving to Moncton? Sam's gonna run her father's motel.

HELEN: You're smart, Sam.

SAM: Yeah, but now Charlie's sore. He acts like I dumped him.

The phone rings. HELEN reaches for it.

SAM: Don't answer that.

HELEN: Why not? …

SAM: Let me do it.

CHARLIE: What gives, Sam? …

SAM: (*picks up the receiver*) Hello … No, it's me, Suitcase … No, he hasn't showed up yet … No, she don't know, either … Look, I told you I'd find him, and I will. You said six-thirty … (*He hangs up*) Charlie, Charlie.

HELEN: Who was it, Sam?

SAM: Someone Charlie oughtn'ta fool with … (*To CHARLIE*) We need to talk, partner. Pronto.

HELEN: Is Charlie in some kind of trouble, Sam? Tell me. I wanta know.

CHARLIE: (*to HELEN*) Don't you have to be at work soon? It's late.

HELEN: It's my night off, remember?

CHARLIE: Well, leave us alone, will you? Sam wants to talk to me.

HELEN: I'm your wife, Charlie. I have a right to know what's going on.

CHARLIE: Just fix me a sandwich, would you? … I won't keep you in the dark, Babe. I promise.

HELEN exits to the kitchen.

SAM: (*sotto voce*) Are you outa your mind, Charlie? Where the hell you been?

CHARLIE: I was with Wanda. What's the big deal?

SAM: You were with Wanda? What, all afternoon?

CHARLIE: Didn't you tell me I owed it to myself? Well, I took your advice.

SAM: What did you pay her with, an I.O.U.?

CHARLIE: What are you driving at? Who was on the phone?

SAM: Who do you think, you stupid bastard? The Hat wants the three Gs you owe him.

CHARLIE: What three Gs? What are you talking about?

SAM: Haven't you heard? Those long shots, Charlie … the two you were supposed to bet … they come in.

CHARLIE: Don't joke like that, Sam!

SAM: It's no joke. Spinning Wheel paid sixteen and change, Jersey Joe, fourteen. He's waiting down at Earl's to collect. I just come from there.

CHARLIE: Sam, I'm a dead man …

SAM: How could you do it, Charlie? You know better than that. You've been around, for Chrissake.

CHARLIE: I never figured he stood a chance. I figured the odds were—

SAM: (*cutting in*) The odds! If the Hat even knew you weren't at the track, know what he'd do to you?

CHARLIE: I know.

SAM: He's one dude you don't mess with, Charlie, ever.

CHARLIE: Christ, I just remembered something.

SAM: What?

CHARLIE: I gotta call Wanda. I gotta cover myself. (*He grabs the telephone book, finds her number, and dials*)

SAM: Know what Jack thinks? He thinks you went on the lam with his winnings.

CHARLIE: He knows me better than that ... C'mon, for Chrissake! Answer! Answer! ... (*Into the phone*) Wanda, it's me, Charlie. Listen, I'm in a bit of a jam. I don't have time to explain. Just do me a favour, will you? If the Hat calls, I wasn't with you this afternoon. I dropped you off and went straight to the track. Got that? ... Thanks, kid. I owe you one. (*He hangs up*) She's cool.

SAM: You shoulda been at Earl's by now. The races're over at four-thirty. He's giving you till six-thirty.

HELEN enters with a sandwich on a plate.

CHARLIE: Six-thirty? Is he crazy? I can't come up with three thousand dollars in forty-five minutes.

HELEN: You owe someone three thousand dollars?

SAM: (*to CHARLIE*) Then you better come up with a damn good story, Charlie, and fast ... Get your coat.

HELEN: Will you tell me what the Christ is going on?

CHARLIE: Not now. I'll explain later. (*To SAM, as he slips on his coat*) What'll I say? My car broke down? I got shut out at the window? He'll know it's bullshit.

SAM: It's the only way, Charlie. He might buy it and give you more time. Anyway, we'll think of something. C'mon.

CHARLIE and SAM exit ... The phone begins to ring. HELEN sets down the plate and watches the phone. It rings and rings.

HELEN: Charlie, what have you done?

Blackout.

Scene Three

The poolhall.

It is unusually quiet in the room, a tense quiet.

JACK THE HAT and BULLDOG are playing pool. AL sits at the counter, watching. EARL stands by the racks, checking the tips of the pool cues.

JACK THE HAT: (*finally*) What time is it, Earl?

EARL: (*looks at his watch*) Ten after six. I may be fast …

AL: He'll be here, Hat. I know Charlie. He wouldn't jack you up.

JACK THE HAT: I wouldn't trust the Pope when it comes to money.

BULLDOG: Want me to go after him, Jack? I'll do it for nothing. As a favour.

JACK THE HAT: I don't need a collector. I handle my own affairs.

BULLDOG: All right. Don't get hot.

AL: He's still got twenty minutes. He'll show.

BULLDOG: He could be halfway to Europe by now.

AL: Not Charlie. He'd never pull that.

BULLDOG: What'd you mean? I know guys who went on the lam for a lot less than three Gs.

JACK THE HAT: Snider only owed two.

AL: (*to JACK THE HAT*) Bulldog still thinks he can make Charlie play him. (*To BULLDOG*) You don't know how stubborn Charlie can be.

BULLDOG: Yeah, well, if Evans thinks he's too good to play me, maybe he won't play at all. Like Earl. He don't play no more, do you, Earl?

Enter CHARLIE and SAM.

AL: See, Hat? I told you he'd show.

EARL crosses behind the counter.

SAM sits beside AL.

CHARLIE moves to the corner of the table and waits for JACK THE HAT to notice him. CHARLIE knows he's being ignored, and that fact in itself is menacing.

JACK THE HAT chalks his cue.

JACK THE HAT: (*finally, turning to CHARLIE*) You took your time, man. Where you been? I don't like waiting.

CHARLIE: I'd like to speak to you, Jack. You know, in private.

BULLDOG: Give him the three Gs and cut the crap.

CHARLIE: Stay outa this, Bulldog! What's it to you?

JACK THE HAT: I'm in the middle of a game, Charlie. What's to talk about? Either you got it or you don't … What was that? I didn't hear you.

CHARLIE: I don't have it …

AL: (*to SAM*) He don't have it?

BULLDOG: Give him to me, Jack. I'll make him cough it up.

JACK THE HAT: I can handle it, Bulldog. It's my beef. (*To CHARLIE*) So what've you been doing all this time? Where you been?

CHARLIE: Walking around.

JACK THE HAT: Walking around? You can do better than that.

CHARLIE: I was afraid to come in, Hat. I knew what you'd think.

JACK THE HAT unscrews his cue and puts the shaft on the table, gripping the butt like a club.

EARL: (*comes out quickly from behind the counter*) Look, Jack, I don't want trouble, understand? You got a beef, take it outside.

JACK THE HAT: Won't be no trouble, Earl. You got my word. Just lock the door. (*EARL doesn't move*) I SAID LOCK THE DOOR, EARL! (*EARL crosses and locks the front door*) Hey, Charlie, why should there be trouble, right? You're gonna reach deeper into your pockets. Right, Charlie?

CHARLIE: I'm not shitting you, Jack. I'm trying to tell you. I couldn't make the bet. If you'd just listen …

SAM: He's giving you the straight goods, Jack.

CHARLIE: Don't get mixed up in it, Sam. This is between the Hat and me … I never made it to the window, Jack. Someone picked my pocket. I had it going through the gate but when I got to the window …

> *JACK THE HAT throws CHARLIE backwards onto the table and presses the butt of the cue on his neck.*

JACK THE HAT: Don't juice me, you mother. What do you take me for? You think you can lay that story on me? I'll rip your heart out.

> *SAM moves to help CHARLIE but is thrown back by BULLDOG. EARL rushes to the table.*

EARL: Let him up, Jack. I said no trouble and I meant it. I got my licence to think of.

> *JACK THE HAT lets CHARLIE up and begins to screw his cue back together.*

JACK THE HAT: Tell me, Charlie. What would you do in my shoes? I go around accepting stories, I'm outa business in no time.

BULLDOG: He'd be a mark for every chiseler in town.

CHARLIE: You never let me finish, Jack. Who's asking you to forget it? All I want is some time. That's all, just time.

JACK THE HAT: (*chalking up*) How much time?

CHARLIE: A week.

BULLDOG: I'd give him three hours, it was me.

JACK THE HAT: All right, Charlie, I'm not hard to get along with. I'll give you till midnight Wednesday.

CHARLIE: That's just two days ...

JACK THE HAT: But I don't want no more stories. You're short even a sawbuck and I won't be responsible.

BULLDOG: (*to CHARLIE*) Speaking for myself ... Know what I hope, you little weasel? I hope you don't come up with it. I hope Jack nails you good!

Blackout.

Scene Four

CHARLIE's flat, later that evening.

HELEN is on the phone. CHARLIE hovers around her, pacing. SAM and AL sit on the sofa.

HELEN: ... I wouldn't ask you, Pete, if it wasn't urgent, you know that ... Listen, I've done more'n my share of double shifts. Have I ever asked for a favour?

CHARLIE: Tell him it's a matter of life and death.

HELEN: I know three grand's a lot of dough, I know that ... All right, I'll hang on ... (*She covers the mouthpiece—To CHARLIE*) One of the girls just came in the office ... He's not gonna give it to me. I can tell. You don't know him, Charlie. He's got the first dollar he ever spent, this guy.

CHARLIE: He's no different than any other mark. Keep firing till you move him.

HELEN: How?

CHARLIE: Tell him it's an advance, not a loan. See if he goes for it.

HELEN: (*back into the phone*) Yeah, Pete, I'm still here ... Okay, I understand. Three grand is outa the question ...

CHARLIE: Shit.

HELEN: Look, can't we just call it an advance? I'm reliable. I won't skip town ... I know it's four month's salary, but I'm in a jam ... All right, then, how much? ... *Two* weeks? That's only three hundred dollars and change.

CHARLIE: What's the good of three hundred?

HELEN: Pete, I need three thousand, not three hundred! ... No, I'll take it ... No, I said I'll take it, Pete.

CHARLIE: Tell him you'll pick it up in the morning.

HELEN: I'll be by in the morning, early, if that's— Thanks, Pete, thanks a lot. (*She hangs up*) Real big of you, you lousy ... (*She looks at* CHARLIE) Sorry, Charlie.

CHARLIE: You did your best.

SAM: (*beat*) What've you got to hock? Anything?

CHARLIE: Piss all. I could sell the TV, and the car might bring me eighty bucks. (*To* HELEN) How much we have in the bank?

HELEN: About four hundred.

SAM: You could get three hundred, maybe four, for the TV, four hundred in the bank, three hundred from Pete, that makes it a thousand, give or take.

CHARLIE: I need two more Gs, Sam.

AL: And you got two days to get it. Great.

HELEN: (*to* CHARLIE) Can't you borrow it?

CHARLIE: Who from? Al? Suitcase?

SAM: I wish I had it, Charlie.

HELEN: What about a loan shark?

SAM: (*to* CHARLIE) That's not a bad idea. Your credit's good. You're known.

CHARLIE: No. No sharks.

AL: Why not?

CHARLIE: What? Twenty per cent interest? That's four hundred dollars a month on two G's.

HELEN: I don't believe it. He's worrying about interest at a time like this ... Charlie, I make close to eight hundred a month. That's twice the interest. One phone call and you can be off the hook for now.

AL: It's a month's grace, Charlie.

HELEN: A lot easier to come up with four hundred next month than two grand in forty-eight hours.

CHARLIE: Don't you get it, Helen? I have to do this myself. I have to break the lock I'm in.

HELEN: Talk to him, Sam. Tell him he's nuts ... The clock's ticking, Charlie. Wake up.

SAM: At least he has front money. He can do a lot with a thousand bucks and the right mark.

HELEN: Sam, you've gotta help him. You can't run out on him now. He needs you.

CHARLIE: He's not running out on me.

HELEN: He's lost his game, Sam ... Did he tell you? The Hat beat him twelve straight, and he's not half the player Charlie is.

AL: Yeah, well, why do you think he's in this jam?

HELEN: What does that mean?

CHARLIE: Nothing. Forget it.

HELEN: No. I wanta know what he meant by that. Where does he get off blaming me?

CHARLIE: (*to AL*) See what you started?

HELEN: How's it my fault, Al? Did I forget the daily double? Did I spend the afternoon in a bar? Did I forget the time?

AL: No.

HELEN: So, Al, how's it my fault?

CHARLIE: Get off his back ... You want the truth? All right, I wasn't at a bar ... I was with Wanda.

HELEN: Wanda?

CHARLIE: And don't ask me why, you know why.

HELEN: So why did you lie to me, Charlie? Did you think I wouldn't understand? … Under the circumstances I could hardly get upset, could I? … So, Al, that's what you meant, is it? My husband goes with some whore and it's my fault. That the way you see it?

AL: I can understand why he did it.

HELEN: Can you?

CHARLIE: (*to HELEN*) You're getting upset.

HELEN: Well, if you're so damn smart, Al, maybe you can tell me why he's sticking his neck out? Because if I was in the fix Charlie's in, I'd take the first way out: the loan shark. I wouldn't play around.

CHARLIE: Who's playing? I gotta get my confidence back or I'm lost. I know it sounds crazy, but I can't take the easy way out. Somehow I gotta do it on my own.

HELEN: You're not listening, Charlie. There are *two* days left. That's all. Forty-eight hours. And you're expecting a *miracle*?

    Blackout.

Scene Five

The poolhall. Early the next evening.

EARL is mopping the washroom floor. MCKEE, early thirties, stands at the urinal, taking a piss.

AL sits at the counter, sipping a coffee. He watches CHARLIE who is behind the counter, dialing the phone.

AL: You sure this guy's got money, Charlie? He don't look it.

CHARLIE: I'm sure. Just before you came in, I asked him to change a fifty. The silly bastard's got a wad of hundreds … (*Into the phone*) Sam? Look, we've got ourselves a live one. Shoot for a thousand right away … Earl? He don't like it much so I cut him in for a piece … Okay, give me ten minutes. (*He hangs up, comes out from behind the counter, and begins to rack up the balls*)

> *In the washroom, MCKEE is now washing his hands. He uses a paper towel, then turns to EARL.*

MCKEE: Hey, you know when the Hat comes in? He still hang out here?

EARL: Why? You a friend of his?

MCKEE: We've done business together, yeah.

EARL: He didn't say. You never know with the Hat. He might come in. Then again, he might not. (*He goes on mopping*)

MCKEE: Thanks. I'll wait. (*He exits the washroom*)

> *CHARLIE is still racking up balls as MCKEE approaches the table.*

CHARLIE: How much you wanta play for? I'm easy.

MCKEE: Depends. How good are you?

CHARLIE: Not too good.

43

MCKEE: (*as* CHARLIE *selects a cue*) You must be good to say that … Besides, this's your room. I oughta get ten or fifteen points for that.

CHARLIE: (*powdering his hands*) Forget it. We play even or we don't play. Now how much?

MCKEE: (*selects a cue*) Okay. How about twenty?

CHARLIE: Sure. Twenty's good. (*Each man puts a twenty-dollar bill in the corner pocket.* CHARLIE *flips a dime on the table*) Call it.

MCKEE: Tails.

CHARLIE: You break.

> MCKEE *breaks. By this time,* EARL *has finished mopping the floor. He switches off the light and exits the washroom.*

CHARLIE: Where you from?

MCKEE: Kitchener. Ever been there?

CHARLIE: Not lately.

EARL: (*crossing to the counter*) I was there once. I took my pants to the cleaners and they come back with a crease down the sides of the legs.

MCKEE: (*to* CHARLIE) Is he for real?

CHARLIE: He used to be one of the best players in the country till they busted his hands.

MCKEE: Who's they?

CHARLIE: Certain people.

MCKEE: Why'd they do that?

CHARLIE: He owed six hundred dollars.

MCKEE: For that they broke his hands?

CHARLIE: For less they'll kill you.

MCKEE: Can't he play anymore?

44

CHARLIE: No ... Never touches a cue now. Hasn't for years.

MCKEE: (*beat*) Hey, you get much action here? You know, big action?

CHARLIE: Some. Why?

MCKEE: Just wondered.

CHARLIE: You want action, you shoulda been here yesterday. Some dude come in called Suitcase Sam. Ever hear of him? Carries his money in a suitcase.

MCKEE: What is he, loaded?

CHARLIE: Yeah. His picture's in every room in the country.

MCKEE: Never heard of him.

CHARLIE: His old man's a millionaire. Tries to keep Suitcase outa the poolhalls ... They say he stuffs up the holes in his shoes with hundred-dollar bills.

MCKEE: You gotta be kidding.

CHARLIE: You musta heard of him. He's famous.

MCKEE: You think he'll be back?

CHARLIE: Sorry, friend, he's mine. I took five hundred off him yesterday, and there's twenty times that in his suitcase ... So what do you do in Kitchener?

MCKEE: Me? I make candles.

CHARLIE: Candles?

MCKEE: Yeah. Can't you smell them? Here, smell my arm.

CHARLIE: I'll take your word for it.

MCKEE: Smell it. (*CHARLIE sniffs*) That's frankincense. Another bad one's musk.

> *Enter BULLDOG. He crosses and sits at the counter. AL immediately rises and crosses to the bench with his coffee.*

45

MCKEE: (*continuing*) The smell gets in your hair, the wallpaper, the furniture. I'm always blowing dye outa my nose, every colour of the rainbow. Man, if my house ever caught fire, there's so much wax there it'd take weeks to burn down. One big Christmas candle, you know.

CHARLIE: What're you doing in Toronto?

MCKEE: Delivering an order.

CHARLIE: You do a big business at Christmas?

MCKEE: Yeah. The rest of the year we make the candles, and Christmas we fill the orders.

CHARLIE: So how's business?

MCKEE: Man, I'm up to my ears in debt, that's how good it is. Had a guy come in last month and sign a purchase order for twenty thousand candles. So I went to the bank, took out a loan. Fifteen thousand dollars. For materials, you know? Now the guy phones and says cancel, he's bankrupt. And now the bank wants the money back …

CHARLIE: Too bad.

MCKEE: Figured I'd deal a little. Maybe score from the Hat. I've done business with him before.

BULLDOG: Score what? The Hat's a gambler, not a pusher. (*To EARL*) The man's a narc. I can smell a narc a mile off.

CHARLIE: That's frankincense, Bulldog.

MCKEE: (*to BULLDOG*) Get serious, man. I'm no narc … I even did time for grass.

BULLDOG: Looks like a hairdresser, don't he, Earl? Even walks like one.

MCKEE: Hey, look, man …

AL: Cut the crap, Bulldog. He says the Hat knows him.

BULLDOG: Bet he hangs out at the steambath.

CHARLIE: Hey, Earl, do something, will you? We're trying to play here.

EARL: (*to BULLDOG*) Come on, ease up, will you? This's getting to be a habit.

MCKEE: (*to BULLDOG*) I don't know what your problem is, man, but watch what you call me.

BULLDOG: What'll you do? Scratch my eyes out?

CHARLIE: (*to MCKEE*) Don't let him get to you. He's just a knocker.

> *Enter JACK THE HAT.*

BULLDOG: Hey, Jack, you know this man? He says you did business together once.

MCKEE: Remember me, Jack? Last summer in Kitchener? … McKee?

JACK THE HAT: Sure. I remember you. (*To BULLDOG*) He's okay. (*Then*) Anybody call, Earl?

EARL: Not since you left.

MCKEE: You sticking around, Hat? I'd like to do some business.

JACK THE HAT: Sure, I'll be around … How you making out, Charlie? Getting it together?

CHARLIE: I'm about to, Jack, if I don't get hammered. (*He nods towards BULLDOG*) I wish you'd see that I don't.

JACK THE HAT: (*to BULLDOG*) Just so we understand each other. He comes up short, I'm the one loses, not him.

> *Enter SUITCASE SAM. He wears an old raccoon coat, a fur hat with flaps over the ears, and wire-rimmed spectacles with one lens missing. He carries an old cardboard suitcase covered in travel stickers.*

(*NOTE: During the ensuing hustle, he never removes his hat or coat*).

CHARLIE: Don't look now, McKee, but my gravy train just rolled in.

MCKEE: Is that him?

CHARLIE: In the flesh … He's given away more dough than the United Appeal. And he's all mine.

> *JACK THE HAT grins and sits at the counter, watching. He takes a swig from a silver flask.*

SAM: (*crosses to the counter—To EARL*) Know what, Mister? I don't think you're one bit funny.

EARL: (*caught off guard*) What? …

SAM: That horse you said to bet on today? Seabiscuit? Someone told me he'd been dead for thirty years.

EARL: (*laughing*) He has been, but he's better than the ones that're running.

CHARLIE: Hey, Suitcase. How you doing? Back for more?

SAM: I remember you.

CHARLIE: Sure you do. I'm the guy you beat yesterday.

SAM: I didn't beat you. You beat me. (*He takes a chain and padlock from his coat pocket and chains the suitcase to the leg of the pinball machine*)

CHARLIE: Oh, yeah, I forgot … (*He takes MCKEE aside*) Look, I can win big here, McKee, so take what's in the pocket. It's all yours. (*He begins to rack up the balls*) So where you been, Suitcase? You said five o'clock. I've been waiting.

SAM: I ain't playing you. You're too good.

CHARLIE: Too good? You gotta be kidding. I was just lucky yesterday.

EARL: (*helping rack up the balls—To* SAM) You're the hotshot here.

SAM: I am?

CHARLIE: I'm telling you, Suitcase, it was dumb luck on my part.

SAM: How much you wanta play for, then?

CHARLIE: Five bills a game.

SAM: How much is that?

CHARLIE: Five hundred dollars.

SAM: No, sir. You think I'm stupid, don't you? I'll play you for a thousand a game or nothing.

CHARLIE: Gimme a break, Suitcase. I don't carry that kind of money on me.

SAM: Then I ain't playing you. My dad says you guys are all bums … That's why he's mad at me.

CHARLIE: Look, we finished at five hundred yesterday. I figured I'd give you a chance to recoup. If I win the next game, we'll play for a thousand, okay?

SAM: No. A thousand now or no dice.

CHARLIE: (*leans over to the table*) Well, screw you, and screw your old man. (*He sends the balls caroming. Then he puts his cue back on the rack*)

MCKEE: (*to* CHARLIE) Hey, let me play him. I've got a thousand dollars.

CHARLIE: Bull.

SAM: Who is this guy? I ain't seen him before.

MCKEE: (*takes out his wallet—To* CHARLIE) Man, I got close to three on me. I just delivered an order to the Kiwanis. Look. (*He shows* CHARLIE *the money*) You believe me now? (*He crosses to* SAM *and opens his wallet*) Will you play me?

SAM: Not 'less you give me points. I always get points. (*Meaning CHARLIE*) He gave me fifty.

CHARLIE: Fifty's too many. He'll give you thirty-five.

SAM: Oh, no. He probably shoots better'n you, and you gave me fifty.

CHARLIE: You told me yesterday you liked to gamble. Take forty.

SAM: Okay. Forty.

> *As SAM gets his thousand dollars from the suitcase, MCKEE antes up. ... CHARLIE takes the money. He glances at JACK THE HAT and smiles. JACK THE HAT touches the brim of his hat, a gesture of encouragement.*

BULLDOG: (*to JACK THE HAT*) Look at him. He thinks he's gonna come up with the dough.

JACK THE HAT: I think he might.

BULLDOG: Yeah, well, I don't.

CHARLIE: (*having counted the money*) It's all there, gents. Twenty beautiful hundred-dollar bills. I'll hold it, okay?

SAM: (*selecting a cue*) Oh, no. You made me pay for the table after you beat me yesterday. (*He points at AL*) Let him hold it.

CHARLIE: (*to AL*) You mind?

AL: No. Sure. (*He takes the money*)

CHARLIE: (*to SAM*) I hope McKee racks your ass.

MCKEE: (*flips a dime on the table*) Call it.

SAM: Heads.

MCKEE: You break.

> *SAM deliberately breaks badly, hitting the blue ball.*

CHARLIE: Nice shot, Suitcase.

The game continues, SAM shooting badly.

BULLDOG: Know what I think, Hat? I think there oughta be a law to protect some people from themselves.

MCKEE: Jack, can't you do something? He's gonna blow it for me … This ain't nickels and dimes, you know.

BULLDOG: What's he supposed to do? Stand me in a corner?

JACK THE HAT: (*to BULLDOG*) Why don't we take a walk? I'll buy you a beer.

BULLDOG: I don't want a beer.

JACK THE HAT: Then let's just take a walk. Earl don't want trouble, do you, Earl?

EARL: You said it, Jack.

JACK THE HAT: You know me, Bulldog. I hate hassles.

BULLDOG: Then don't crowd me.

JACK THE HAT: Who's crowding you? I'm just protecting my interests. You can understand that.

> *Silence. BULLDOG glances from JACK THE HAT to CHARLIE. Then he rises from his stool, brings out his roll.*

BULLDOG: All right, Jack, I'll tell you what I'll do. (*He crosses to the table, counts out three grand, and slaps it on the table*) It's all there. Three grand … Now he owes it to me.

CHARLIE: Take that money, Jack, and he'll be free to hammer me.

MCKEE: What's happening?

AL: He'll make the deadline two hours, Hat. Charlie's only in this 'cause he tried to do you a favour.

> *JACK THE HAT considers.*

JACK THE HAT: (*finally—to BULLDOG*) I'll take it if you let the deadline stand. Midnight tomorrow.

BULLDOG: Sure, Jack. I'm a reasonable man. (*He scoops up the money and hands it to JACK THE HAT*)

JACK THE HAT: (*counting it*) All right, you two settle it. I only want what's owed me.

CHARLIE: Thought you always went for the long shots, Hat?

JACK THE HAT: Only at the track, Charlie. This is business … (*To MCKEE*) Hey, you. What's your name?

MCKEE: McKee.

JACK THE HAT: You still wanta talk, McKee, see me across the street. I'll be in the Jade Palace. (*He exits*)

MCKEE: (*looks around*) Hey, let's get back to the game … What is this? Are we playing pool or not?

BULLDOG: Can't wait to lose your socks, can you?

MCKEE: Who? Me?

BULLDOG: I don't see another hick in the room … Don't you know you ain't gonna win? That man's gonna crack you out.

CHARLIE: Yeah, sure,

BULLDOG: The spot's gonna beat you, stupid. That man could spot you fifty and still clobber you.

MCKEE: Get serious, man.

BULLDOG: Don't you see? You're being conned, taken, hustled. Want it any plainer than that?

MCKEE: Hustled?

BULLDOG: They're partners, dummy. Suitcase could brush his teeth with Pepsodent and still run the table … (*To CHARLIE*) Give him back his dough.

CHARLIE: Goddamn you, Bulldog, we had him all sewed up.

MCKEE: (*slams his cue on the table*) I want my money. Gimme my money.

BULLDOG: (*to MCKEE*) Let this be a lesson to you.

CHARLIE: Give him his money, Al.

> *As AL counts out the bills, SAM removes his cap and puts the cue back in the rack.*

BULLDOG: (*to MCKEE*) Don't let me catch you in here again, you hear? (*MCKEE takes his money, grabs his coat, and dashes for the front door*) Now beat it while you can still walk. The Hat's across the street.

> *MCKEE exits.*

BULLDOG: That wasn't too smart, Earl. You could get heat over that. (*He crosses and gets his hat and coat*)

EARL: Think I wanta see Charlie get his hands busted?

BULLDOG: (*to CHARLIE*) Lemme tell you a story, Evans. When I was little, a kid tried to cheat me at marbles. So I stuck my knife in his hand. They kicked me outa school for that. The punk was *cheating*, but they kicked *me* out. Go figure. (*He exits*)

SAM: Get out now, Charlie. Go home and pack your stuff.

CHARLIE: Where would I go, Sam?

SAM: Look, we'd planned on leaving Thursday, Candy and me. But we could easily go tomorrow ... We could put you up down there. He'd never find you.

EARL: He'd find him. Guys like Bulldog don't give up ... Walk in any room in the country, he'd be fingered.

AL: Stay outa the poolrooms, then.

CHARLIE: And what would I do, Al? Pump gas?

AL: You can't shoot pool with your hands in a cast.

CHARLIE: (*angrily*) I'm a pool player, okay? If I let him take my game away, I might as well hand him my head on a stick.

EARL: Take it easy, we're on your side ... Look, Charlie, if you need a place to lay low, I got a room upstairs ...

AL: Besides, you can still go to a shark.

CHARLIE: I already said no to that, Al. No sharks ... I need to come up with the money myself ... If I could just find another mark ...

EARL: Not in here, Charlie.

SAM: (*to CHARLIE*) Not every mark's got a bankroll like McKee. Might take weeks to get that lucky again.

CHARLIE: Wait a minute ... Wanda.

SAM: Wanda? What about her?

CHARLIE: Why didn't I think of it? She's got a new john. He oughta still be in town. She said the guy was loaded ... Sam, if I could set something up for tonight, could I count on you?

SAM: Only if you promise you'll go to a shark if it don't work out.

CHARLIE: All right, you got my word ... Sam, I think I know just how to move this guy. I think I've got an idea ... Can I use your phone, Earl?

EARL: Help yourself. But just remember, Charlie. No more moves like that in my place. Is that understood?

Blackout.

ACT TWO

Scene One

CHARLIE's flat. (NOTE: The TV has been struck).

HELEN is tidying up ... CHARLIE and SAM burst in, SAM carrying a bottle of scotch in a brown paper bag.

CHARLIE: Did you call the club? Did you tell Pete you weren't coming in?

HELEN: He was sore, Charlie. Not that I blame him. He just gave me a two week advance ... What's this all about?

CHARLIE: The Hat's outa the picture. Bulldog paid him off ... Now I owe him the three G's.

HELEN: Bulldog?

SAM: We had a mark all lined up, too.

HELEN: Maybe I should talk to him, Charlie. I'll do it, if you want me to.

CHARLIE: Just put on a dress. We're having company. And get some glasses from the kitchen. He'll be here any minute.

HELEN: Wait a minute, slow down ... Who'll be here any minute?

CHARLIE: Don't hit the roof, okay? I found another mark ... The thing is, he thinks he's coming to a party.

HELEN: A party? What kind of party?

CHARLIE: An orgy.

HELEN: An orgy?

CHARLIE: It's just the bait to get him here … He's a rich freak. Some client of Wanda's. She's bringing him.

HELEN: What? Wanda's coming here?

SAM: She's not in on it. She has no idea it's a setup.

HELEN: Forget it, Charlie. I don't want that woman in my house. I mean it.

CHARLIE: I already called her. It's all arranged … Look, this guy's an answer to our prayers. You wanta queer it on account of Wanda? Use your head.

HELEN: (*beat*) What does he expect me to do?

CHARLIE: Relax. He has a plane to catch. We'll tap him before he's finished his first scotch.

HELEN exits.

SAM: I don't know about this, Charlie. You know it's risky, don't you?

CHARLIE: What? Bringing him here?

SAM: Yeah. It mighta been better to rent a room. He could bring steam on you.

CHARLIE: The guy's got a family, Sam. He'd have to explain Wanda. Somehow I don't see him doing that, do you?

HELEN returns, wearing a red chiffon dress. She sits at the vanity and brushes her hair.

HELEN: What're you gonna do? Get him in a card game?

CHARLIE: We don't have time for that. No, it's gotta be something quick. We figured the boxes … At some point I want you to go to the liquor store. Take Wanda with you.

HELEN: What for?

CHARLIE: We have to get her outa here while we dust him. She sees we're hustling her trick, she'll blow the whistle. (*The buzzer sounds*) That's them, now. Remember, keep her out as long as you can, understand?

HELEN: How? The liquor store's a block away. How long can I drag my feet?

CHARLIE: You'll think of something... Now hurry up, they're here. (*He exits down the hall*)

SAM: He's almost outa moves, Helen. Don't blow it for him.

HELEN: All he has to do is phone a shark. You're his friend, Sam. Why don't you talk to him?

> *CHARLIE enters, followed by WANDA and GREG, an expensively dressed businessman in his late forties. WANDA wears a fur coat.*

CHARLIE: Greg, this is Helen. Helen, Greg.

GREG: (*impressed*) Hello, there.

HELEN: Hi.

CHARLIE: (*to HELEN*) And you know Wanda.

HELEN: Sure. I know her.

WANDA: Hiya, hon.

HELEN: It's been a long time. You're looking good.

WANDA: You think so? I just had my appendix out.

CHARLIE: (*to GREG*) Sam here's an old friend. He just happened to drop by.

GREG: The more the merrier I always say … Glad to meet you, Sam.

SAM: Any friend of Wanda's a friend of mine.

CHARLIE: Here, lemme take your coats. (*He does*) Look, sit down, why don't you? I'll pour the drinks.

HELEN: I'll get the glasses.

GREG: (*to HELEN as she exits*) You know, I'm going to hate to get on that plane tonight. I just know it.

HELEN: (*tightly smiling*) Be right back. (*She exits*)

WANDA: Don't drool on the lady, Greg. It wrinkles the chiffon.

> *GREG sits on the sofa beside WANDA. SAM takes a chair from the vanity and sits.*

CHARLIE: (*to GREG*) Wanda tells me you're from Detroit. (*He sits on the arm of the armchair*)

GREG: That's right, Motor City.

CHARLIE: What do you think of T.O.?

GREG: Well, Chuck, if I had to choose a city and I couldn't live in Marrakesh, I just might settle here. (*He smiles at WANDA*)

WANDA: (*to CHARLIE*) He's sweet, ain't he?

GREG: You guys do much travelling?

CHARLIE: Some.

SAM: I just flew back from Miami.

GREG: Oh? What kind of business you in?

SAM: What kind? ... The motel business.

WANDA: Since when?

CHARLIE: Didn't you hear, Wanda? Candy inherited a motel down east... He wasn't in Miami on business, were you, Sam? (*To GREG*) He was on his honeymoon.

GREG: (*to SAM*) First time married?

CHARLIE: Sam's a three-time loser, Greg. The first time he was only twenty.

WANDA: Way too young.

SAM: The day I got hitched, I had my shoes shined, and the guy at the stand asked me why I wasn't in school.

Everybody laughs.

CHARLIE: I know what we need: music. (*He switches on the record player*)

HELEN returns with a tray on which are five glasses and a bowl of ice cubes. She sets it down on the coffee table.

CHARLIE pours drinks.

CHARLIE: How do you take it, Greg?

GREG: Straight.

WANDA: I need to stretch my legs. (*To HELEN*) Why don't you sit beside Greg? He won't bite. (*She rises and stands in the doorway, watching SAM*)

HELEN sits beside GREG.

GREG: Wanda tells me you're a dancer.

HELEN: Actually, a stripper.

GREG: I haven't seen a stripper since Virginia "Ding Dong" Bell. In those days all the girls were built like you-know-what.

HELEN: Some still are.

GREG: You're very attractive, Helen. My wife does TV commercials, and she can't hold a candle to you.

CHARLIE: No kidding? Your wife's on TV?

WANDA: You never told me that, Greg. What commercials? Maybe I seen her in one.

GREG: I was an actor myself once. That's how we met. We made a porno flick together in L.A. *Piranha Girls*.

WANDA: Greg, I swear I never know when you're pulling my leg. (*To SAM*) *Piranha Girls*!

CHARLIE: (*quickly*) Damn, we're almost outa scotch. Hold down the fort, would you, Helen, while I pop down to the Liquor Store?

HELEN: Never mind, I'll go.

GREG: Don't send the lady out in the cold, Chuck. It's not that important.

HELEN: I don't mind. The walk'll do me good … Wanda, would you keep me company? It's just up the block.

WANDA: It's chilly out there.

HELEN: We'll only be a minute.

GREG: Go with the lady, Wanda. In this neighbourhood she might need protection. (*He slips her some bills*)

WANDA: What am I, a nursemaid? … Keep it on the fire, Sammy. This may be your lucky night. … Come on, Helen. Let's blow this pop-stand. (*She and HELEN exit*)

CHARLIE: (*pours more scotch*) Hey, Greg, tell me the truth. Did you really act in a porno film?

GREG: Hell, that's nothing. I made it once in a Cessna flying to Las Vegas. Boy, that was flight.

SAM: Vegas is the one place I'd like to visit.

CHARLIE: (*to GREG*) You've really been around, haven't you? I thought you might turn out to be some guy with shiny pants and a hairpiece.

SAM: Hey, Charlie, how 'bout a game of cards? Just till the women get back?

CHARLIE: Naw, cards bore me.

SAM: (*to GREG*) He's scared I'll beat him.

CHARLIE: Dream on, buddy.

SAM: I saw a game the other day. I could show you that.

CHARLIE: Greg don't wanta see your stupid games, do you, Greg?

SAM: We got time. It'll only take a minute.

GREG: Sure. Go ahead.

SAM: (*to CHARLIE*) Got any wooden matchboxes? You know, the little ones.

CHARLIE: I think I do.

SAM: Bring me three, if you have them. (*CHARLIE exits. SAM cleans off the coffee table. To GREG*) Charlie's always beating me at poker. Maybe tonight I can win some back. (*He takes a Kleenex from a box on the vanity. He rips off a piece, wets it with his tongue, and rolls it into a small pea-sized ball. Then he kneels behind the coffee table*)

CHARLIE: (*enters*) These what you want? (*He hands SAM three small wooden matchboxes*)

SAM: Perfect. (*He empties the matchboxes, discards the outsides, and turns the boxes bottom up on the table*) All set.

GREG: That looks like the old shell game.

SAM: Really?

GREG: Yeah, I saw it once at a carnival. The guy used three walnut shells and a pea.

SAM: I wouldn't know 'bout that. I saw two kids do it for the first time last week. (*He puts the ball under one of the boxes and shuffles the boxes slowly*) All right, Charlie. Where's the ball?

CHARLIE: What? Are you kidding? Right there.

SAM: (*lifts the box*) You're right. Let's try again. (*He shuffles slightly faster this time, yet still not fast enough so that GREG will lose sight of the box containing the ball*) All right, Charlie. Let's see how you do this time.

CHARLIE: That's easy. This one.

GREG: You're wrong, Chuck. It's that one there.

CHARLIE: And I'm telling you it's this one. I'd bet my last dollar on it.

SAM: A hundred bucks says you need your eyes checked.

CHARLIE: (*to GREG*) This is how he loses his shirt ... Okay, Sam. A hundred bucks. I hope you can afford it.

SAM: I can afford it. I just won a bundle at the track. (*He and CHARLIE each put a hundred dollars on the table*)

CHARLIE: Go ahead.

GREG: Don't say I didn't warn you.

> SAM *lifts the box* GREG *had pointed to. The ball is there.*

CHARLIE: Dammit, Greg, you were right. I shoulda listened. (*To SAM*) The guy's got twenty-twenty. (*To SAM*) Let's do it again.

SAM: No, I don't wanta take advantage.

CHARLIE: Get serious. I wanta win back my hundred. (*He lays down two hundred dollars*) One hundred, two hundred ... Shuffle.

SAM: You're the boss. (*He shuffles fast. From this point on, SAM is completely controlling the game. In theory, whenever he shuffles, he palms the ball. If he wants someone to win, all he has to do is let the ball drop out of his hand as he lifts the box. However, to simplify things, all that is needed is for one of the three boxes to be marked so that the actors know the ball is under that particular box at all times. Therefore, the only time SAM has to palm the ball is on the very last shuffle*) Which one?

CHARLIE: Which one, Greg? Gimme a hand.

GREG: Try that one.

CHARLIE: Right. I'll say this one.

> SAM *lifts the box. The ball is there.*

SAM: No fair, Greg.

CHARLIE: (*to GREG*) What do you know? We won. Hey, partner. (*He slaps GREG's hand*) Let's see. There's four hundred on the table, right? Let's shoot the works. I feel lucky.

SAM: (*laying down four hundred dollars*) Next time no prompting, Greg. Unless, of course, you wanta get in on the game. That's different.

CHARLIE: What? You'll take us both on?

SAM: Call me Fearless.

CHARLIE: What do you say, Greg? With your eyes, we can't miss … The bundle he won at the track, it'll only burn a hole in his pocket.

GREG: All right, I'll give it a try. (*He takes out his wallet*) Let's see. I'm in for half, right? (*He hands CHARLIE two hundred dollars. CHARLIE takes the vanity chair and sits at one end of the coffee table*)

SAM: Okay, you guys. You ready for this? (*He shuffles the boxes fast*)

CHARLIE: (*to GREG*) Any idea where it is? I'm lost.

GREG: I'm not sure … I think it's this one.(*To SAM*) Yeah, this one.

CHARLIE: Okay, I'll go with that.

> SAM *lifts the box. It's empty.*

GREG: Damn.

SAM: Sorry, gents. You lose. (*He lifts another box to reveal the ball*) I got eight hundred here, Charlie. Wanta shoot for another four?

CHARLIE: (*checks his wallet*) No. Helen would kill me.

SAM: (*laughs*) This makes up for what I lost at poker.

CHARLIE: (*to GREG*) Don't you just hate a guy that gloats? … All right, smartass, four hundred. (*He lays down *the money and sits*) You've been lucky so far. It can't last.

SAM: You in, Greg?

GREG: Sure. Why not? (*Puts in his money*)

SAM: All right, now. Keep your eye on the little box, and Uncle Sam will work his magic fingers. (*He shuffles fast*) There. Name the box, gents.

CHARLIE: I say it's this one.

GREG: No, I'm pretty sure it's that one.

CHARLIE: Okay, I'll go along with Greg.

SAM lifts the box. It is empty.

CHARLIE: Shit.

GREG: I could've sworn ...

SAM lifts another box to reveal the ball.

CHARLIE: Well, that wipes me out. (*To GREG*) I still think you can beat this guy. You're only down six hundred.

GREG: I think I'll just bet a hundred this time. I want to watch more closely ... (*He puts down a hundred dollars*)

SAM: Playing it safe, huh? (*He shuffles fast but not too fast*) Call it.

GREG: That one.

SAM lifts the box. The ball is there.

SAM: Shit.

CHARLIE: (*to GREG*) Too bad you didn't bet higher ... (*To SAM*) He's got your number, pal.

SAM: Some friend.

Offstage, we hear a door open and close, and HELEN and WANDA laughing.

GREG: Looks like the ladies are back.

SAM: That was quick.

CHARLIE: Just when the game was starting to get interesting.

> *Enter HELEN and WANDA. HELEN carries two bottles of scotch.*

WANDA: We're back.

HELEN: Did you miss us?

CHARLIE: The way you two were laughing, it sounded like you had a good time out there.

HELEN: Wanda missed her honeybun, didn't you, Wanda? Kept reminding me Greg has a plane to catch.

WANDA: She's crazy, Charlie. How many drinks did Helen have? One? One little drink, and she's flirting with the cop at the Liquor Store. You shoulda seen her. Hanging onto his arm, calling him cute, this big harness bull with a chin like Dick Tracy. I had to practically pry her away ... Anyway, we got the scotch. (*She flings her coat on the floor*) Let's party.

CHARLIE: Greg and Sam wanta finish up, then we'll party ... (*To WANDA*) Why don't you pour Greg a scotch?

WANDA: My pleasure.

> *HELEN crosses and stands beside GREG. She rests her hand on his shoulder.*

HELEN: (*teasingly*) What're you doing, Greg? You're not taking advantage of Sam, are you?

GREG: Taking advantage? I'm down five hundred ... Sit here beside me. Maybe you'll bring me luck.

WANDA: Watch out for Sammy, Greg. He's a lot smarter than he looks. (*She hands GREG his scotch*)

SAM: (*laughs*) I beg to differ, doll.

CHARLIE: Yeah, well, his luck's about to run out.

HELEN: (*to GREG*) How much you betting?

CHARLIE: How 'bout four hundred, Greg? You win, you're only a hundred in the hole.

GREG: Sounds good. (*He lays down four hundred dollars*) Let's see if I can't nail him.

SAM: Here goes. (*He shuffles, GREG again watching intently*) Too fast for you?

> *But a change has come over GREG.*

GREG: Tell you what, Sam. Let's reverse this thing. You tell *me* which box the ball is under.

CHARLIE: (*knowing something's wrong*) That doesn't make sense, Greg. He knows where it is.

SAM: You wanta lose the four hundred?

GREG: On second thought, let me do it for you. Is it this one? (*He lifts a box*) No. (*Lifts another*) No ... Must be the last box. (*Lifts the box*) Well, what do you know? It's not there, either.

WANDA: Hey, what gives?

GREG: (*to SAM*) It's in your hand, isn't it? You palm it when you shuffle. There's no way I win unless you want me to ... The whole thing was a setup.

WANDA: A setup?

CHARLIE: (*snatching up the money*) Okay, the party's over. It was nice knowing you, Greg. (*To WANDA*) Better get him to the airport before he misses his plane.

WANDA: You mean they were cheating?

GREG: I suppose you didn't know? ... What the hell you take me for, Wanda? I'm slow to catch on but not that slow.

WANDA: Greg, I swear I wasn't in on it. Sam, tell him I wasn't. Charlie, tell him.

CHARLIE: She wasn't. She had nothing to do with it.

WANDA: See, Greg? I had no idea. Honestly, honey, I thought—

GREG: (*cutting her off—to CHARLIE*) You owe me nine hundred dollars. Let's have it.

CHARLIE: Sorry, pal. No can do.

WANDA: Give him back his dough, Charlie. Please.

GREG: I'm warning you. I'll call the police.

CHARLIE: There's the phone. Help yourself.

HELEN: Greg doesn't wanta bring trouble on himself, do you, Greg?

WANDA: (*to GREG*) She's right, hon. Let's just go. Let's get outa here. (*Takes his arm*)

GREG: (*brushing her off*) Get away from me...Christ, I should've known better than to trust a hooker. (*He slips on his coat—To HELEN*) As for you, I give you full marks. You even had an old cynic like me convinced. (*He exits*)

WANDA: Greg! Wait! Greg! (*She slips on her coat*) You bastards! I'll get you for this, Charlie. Greg's one in a million, and now you've gone and screwed it up. (*She exits*)

CHARLIE: (*to HELEN*) Why didn't you keep her out? We had him just where we wanted.

HELEN: She's not stupid. She woulda suspected something if I'd stalled much longer.

CHARLIE: We had him in the palm of our hands, didn't we, Sam?

SAM: Just like old times.

HELEN: Yeah, well, you're still short eleven hundred, Charlie … Now will you phone a loan shark?

CHARLIE: I've still got one more day.

HELEN: No. You promised to call a shark if this didn't work out.

SAM: We're holding you to it.

CHARLIE: One more day, Sam …

SAM: No. Now pick up the phone, Charlie, or I'll call myself and borrow it.

HELEN: At least you'll have Bulldog off your back. That's the most important thing, no matter what you think … Pick up the phone, Charlie.

CHARLIE: All right, already. (*He picks up the phone and begins to dial*)

> *Blackout.*

Scene Two

The poolhall. It is the next day, late afternoon.

*EARL and BULLDOG sit at the counter, playing gin.
JACK THE HAT and AL are playing pool.*

BULLDOG: (*snapping his fingers*) Hey, you asleep or what?

EARL: Don't rush me ... (*Studies his cards*) What'll you
do, Bulldog, if Charlie don't come up with the
dough tonight?

BULLDOG: I'll hunt him down.

EARL: Where would you start?

BULLDOG: Don't worry, Earl. I'm a patient man. He'll
have to come up for air sooner or later.

AL: I hope he's in Australia by then.

BULLDOG: Not Evans. He'll be in the city. Some
cockroach hotel with the blinds drawn.

JACK THE HAT: That's a lotta flea-bags.

BULLDOG: Think I'd waste my time looking in hotels?

AL: What'll you do, then?

BULLDOG: I'll do what you do with any weasel. I'll smoke
him out.

AL: (*to JACK THE HAT*) He's proud of breaking legs.

BULLDOG: Listen, a man don't pay what he owes
deserves what he gets. You welch on a bank, they
take away your house. Those are the rules.

Enter CHARLIE.

BULLDOG: Well, if it ain't the weasel ... (*To JACK THE HAT*)
He looks like he lost his best friend, don't he, Jack?
... It's five o'clock, Evans. You got till midnight.

CHARLIE: What the hell gives, Hat? Last night I borrowed
eleven hundred from a shark. I go today to pick it

up, the guy says, Sorry, the Hat put out the word not to give you a nickel. I called around town and got the same answer. I wanta know why.

JACK THE HAT: You figure it out, Charlie. You're a bright boy.

CHARLIE: Figure what out, Jack?

JACK THE HAT: You shouldn't have screwed me, Charlie. I don't like it.

CHARLIE: (*to AL*) What's he talking about?

AL: Search me, Charlie. The first I heard of it.

BULLDOG: (*to CHARLIE, meaning JACK*) What do you take him for, a mooch? He oughta poke your eye out.

JACK THE HAT: That story you gave me how you were ripped off at the track? Remember that?

CHARLIE: What about it?

JACK THE HAT: You were never at the races, Charlie. Wanda called me this morning ... So don't go telling me stories, okay?

CHARLIE: Gimme a break, Hat. You know the spot I'm in ... I only agreed to run the bet out as a favour to you.

JACK THE HAT: And did you do it? Did you do me that simple favour? No. You took my half a yard and spent it. So don't ask me for favours now, Charlie.

CHARLIE: All right, Jack. I admit I made a mistake ... But what would you've done in my shoes? What?

JACK THE HAT: You not only lied to me, Charlie, you cost Wanda her trick. That's another piece of change I won't see on time ... A guy messes with me, Charlie, I don't like it.

AL: I'll borrow the money, Charlie. You can pay me back.

JACK THE HAT: (*to AL*) Anyone comes to this man's aid answers to me, understand? ... That goes for you, Suitcase, anyone.

Blackout.

Scene Three

The lights come slowly up on the poolhall. It is eight in the evening.

EARL is brushing the table. BULLDOG, cue in hand, stands at the end of the table, waiting for EARL to finish. JACK THE HAT leans against the pinball machine.

BULLDOG: (*meaning EARL*) The man's a real hustler, Jack. He punches my ticket, then brushes the table. He's fulla little moves like that.

EARL: I'm not hustling you, Bulldog. But I have hustled more than pool in my time.

JACK THE HAT: Like what, Earl?

EARL: Well, I'll tell you ... Whenever I was down on my luck, I'd buy a cheap watch and sell it for whatever I could get. The most was seventy-five dollars. Turn the guy's wrist green in a week, but I'd be long gone. It was a good hustle ... (*He turns to BULLDOG just as BULLDOG takes the black ball and the cue ball from the corner pocket and lines up a shot*) "Pardon me, sir." ... (*BULLDOG stops and looks at him*) "Can I talk to you a minute? I have to get back to Yellowknife." One guy even pointed the way. I said, "No, I know how to get there. It's just that I lost my bus ticket, and I gotta get home, my kid's sick. I don't want something for nothing, you understand." (*BULLDOG bends to make the shot*) "You look like an honest man." (*BULLDOG straightens and looks at EARL*) "I have a watch here." (*To JACK THE HAT*) And I'd give him the quick flash. (*He demonstrates, showing his wristwatch*) Just the quick flash, and then it was the story he bought. (*To BULLDOG*) "I have a watch here that my wife bought me, and I was wondering if you could you help me?"

BULLDOG: (*playing along*) "I've got a watch." (*He picks up the cue ball, crosses to the other side of the table, and lines up a shot. EARL follows him*)

EARL: (*just as BULLDOG is about to shoot*) " I can see you have a watch, sir, but I'm new in town." (*BULLDOG straightens and looks at him*) "I don't wanta go to a pawnshop, they just take advantage. If you could lend me, say, thirty dollars, I could take your name and address and you could take my watch, and when I get back home, I'll send you back the money, plus an extra fifteen for being so honest. I know you wouldn't keep my watch. You wouldn't, would you?" (*Exasperated, BULLDOG walks away and chalks his cue. EARL crosses to JACK THE HAT*) So now if he goes for it, I give him the watch and some phoney address ... Worked almost every time.

    Enter WANDA.

EARL: Hiya, kid. You look tired ... Have a bad day? (*He moves behind the counter*)

WANDA: (*crosses to the counter*) I worked so hard today, Earl, I think I busted a stitch. That goddamn Charlie. I've been standing out there in the cold 'cause of him.

JACK THE HAT: What're you doing working the street?

WANDA: I have to, Jack. When I got that sugardaddy, I threw away my book. Now I have to start my business from scratch. That takes time.

JACK THE HAT: That'll teach you to let some trick control you ... How much did you make?

WANDA: I couldn't ask my usual on the street, Jack. They're only charging twenty-five.

JACK THE HAT: I never asked how much you took in.

WANDA: I had eight tricks.

JACK THE HAT: How many?

WANDA: All right, eight and a half, if you count the midget.

JACK THE HAT: I'll take it.

WANDA: All of it?

JACK THE HAT: You owe me three and a half, don't you?

WANDA: Jeez, leave me enough for cab fare, Hat.

JACK THE HAT: (*snaps his fingers*) C'mon, c'mon.

BULLDOG: (*shooting balls*) When she was with me, Jack, I had to frisk her every time she walked in the door.

WANDA: Mind your own business … Hey, Hat, that was a joke about the midget.

JACK THE HAT: Gimme the two hundred … (*WANDA removes the money from her blouse, starts to count it, then hands it to JACK*) You owe me a yard and a half by the weekend.

WANDA: Thanks a lot.

JACK THE HAT: I don't take it now, Wanda, you'll only lose it. Look at it this way: I'm doing you a favour.

WANDA: Some favour. (*To EARL*) One of these days I'm going back to Barrie, and that's it.

EARL: Is that where you're from? … What the hell would you do in Barrie? (*He hands her a shot of whiskey*)

WANDA: I dunno. Buy a little house. Marry some sweet guy who thinks I'm a virgin. Maybe have kids.

> *Enter CHARLIE and SAM. SAM carries his two-piece pool cue in its carrying case.*

WANDA: There they are now, the bastards. You're lucky I'm not a man or I'd paste you both. That was a shitty thing you did last night, Charlie.

CHARLIE: (*crosses to the counter*) I know … I'm sorry, kid. I'll try and make it up to you.

WANDA: How? … I gotta work the street now, 'cause of you. What if I get busted? I've already been in court twice. Once more, they'll probably toss the book at me.

CHARLIE: You know my situation, Wanda. I wouldn't have done it otherwise.

WANDA: Is that supposed to make me feel better? Well, it doesn't.

CHARLIE: … Anyway, you called the Hat and now I can't use a shark. What more do you want, blood?

BULLDOG: If you're still here in four hours, she'll get her wish. (*He slams the black ball into the corner pocket*)

CHARLIE: (*to SAM*) I'll be right back. (*He crosses into the washroom, flicks on the light, and waits*)

JACK THE HAT: Never know what a desperate man will do, Bulldog. Might even knock over a Mac's Milk. (*He starts for the washroom*)

BULLDOG: The man don't have the balls.

JACK THE HAT: Get a guy cornered, he might surprise you. (*He enters the washroom*)

BULLDOG: Did you hear that, Earl? He might surprise me … Give Evans a gun and he'd shoot off his toe. (*He continues shooting*)

CHARLIE: Did you get the piece?

JACK THE HAT: Yeah, but it'll cost you a hundred.

CHARLIE: You said seventy-five.

JACK THE HAT: I had to go outa my way. Take it or leave it.

CHARLIE: Okay, okay. (*He pays him*) Did you bring it with you?

JACK THE HAT: What do you think? (*He removes a gun from his jacket pocket and hands it to* CHARLIE) The serial number's been filed off.

CHARLIE: What about the bullets?

JACK THE HAT: (*hands* CHARLIE *a Ziploc bag containing six bullets*) What're you gonna do? Knock over a store?

CHARLIE: No. It's for protection.

JACK THE HAT: Better shoot to kill, then. No gun's gonna scare off a collector. (*He exits the washroom*)

> CHARLIE *slips the gun inside his waistband. He checks himself out in the mirror, then runs cold water, which he tosses on his face.*

BULLDOG: (*to* EARL) Wanta bet I don't make the next ten blacks?

JACK THE HAT: Ten years ago Earl coulda made the next twenty with one eye shut. Couldn't you, Earl?

EARL: True. I could put more juice on a cue ball than any man in the country.

CHARLIE: You were the best, Earl.

WANDA: Jeez, the way you guys talk. It's only a game, for Chrissake.

SAM: Speaking of which … (*He takes his cue from its case and screws it together*) I'm looking for action, Bulldog. You interested?

BULLDOG: Forget it.

SAM: What's wrong? I've got five hundred.

BULLDOG: Yeah? Whose is it?

WANDA: Don't let him hustle you, Bulldog. I've seen how he operates.

CHARLIE: Give him points, Sam … (*To* BULLDOG) How many you want? Twenty? Thirty?

BULLDOG: What do you take me for? I wouldn't play Suitcase if he gave me fifty ... I'll play you, though.

CHARLIE: Yeah, sure.

SAM: (*as JACK THE HAT puts on his coat*) How 'bout you, Jack? Care for a game?

JACK THE HAT: You're too good, Suitcase.

SAM: Know what the word is, Jack? The word is you only play mooches. Not that I believe it, you understand.

JACK THE HAT: Yeah, well, take a look at me, a good look. (*He gestures to his clothes*) How do you think I got all this? From letting myself get hustled?

SAM: Okay, I'll spot you.

JACK THE HAT: How many?

SAM: Fifteen.

JACK THE HAT: I'll take what Charlie offered Bulldog: thirty.

SAM: Twenty. That's as high as I'll go. I'm not that good.

JACK THE HAT: Screw it, then.

CHARLIE: Give him thirty, Sam.

SAM: Okay, thirty.

> *JACK THE HAT removes his coat and gets out his cue. SAM crosses to BULLDOG who is still shooting balls.*

SAM: I've got some action here, Bulldog. Do you mind? (*Meaning "Can I have the table?"*)

BULLDOG: I'm busy.

CHARLIE: (*to EARL*) They're playing for a hundred a game.

EARL: Be reasonable, Bulldog. If you wanted to play for serious money, you wouldn't like waiting around, would you?

WANDA: It's Bulldog's table. He was here first.

BULLDOG: This ain't the only room. Let him go somewhere else.

EARL: (*as BULLDOG is about to shoot*) I ain't telling you, Bulldog, I'm asking you. (*He picks up the cue ball*) I need the table, okay?

BULLDOG: I won't forget this, Earl ... Punch my ticket off.

EARL: I'll take care of your ticket.

SAM: Thanks, man.

> *CHARLIE, SAM, and EARL help rack up the balls. SAM and JACK THE HAT put a hundred each in the corner pocket.*

JACK THE HAT: (*flips a dime on the table*) Call it.

SAM: Tails.

JACK THE HAT: You break.

SAM: (*chalking up*) Cue ball fouls?

JACK THE HAT: Sure.

WANDA: (*to CHARLIE*) I hope the Hat takes him to the cleaners. Then you'll know how it feels.

> *As SAM goes to break, BULLDOG casually switches on the radio.*

SAM: Turn that thing off, will you?

> *EARL does.*

JACK THE HAT: Whatever you think you're doing, Bulldog, it won't work. So cool it.

BULLDOG: I won't make a sound, Jack. Word of honour.

> *SAM breaks.*

> *BULLDOG pays EARL for a bag of potato chips. He sits at the counter beside WANDA.*

BULLDOG rips open the bag.

Both SAM *and* JACK THE HAT *stare at him.*

BULLDOG: What?

Blackout.

Scene Four

CHARLIE's flat, ten-thirty that night.

HELEN is just finishing packing CHARLIE's suitcase.

Enter CHARLIE and SAM.

CHARLIE: What're you doing home? It's only ten-thirty. (*He tosses his coat over a chair*)

HELEN: I was too upset to work ... Look, I managed to get a stag for next week. Plus Pete's giving me two double shifts on Thursday and Friday.

CHARLIE: Did you hit up the girls at the club?

HELEN: Yeah. They're all broke, as usual ... Did you have any luck at Earl's?

SAM: I made another four bills.

CHARLIE: Sam beat the Hat four games ... then Jack froze him.

HELEN: That means we're still seven short.

SAM: I tried to keep it close ... but he caught on.

CHARLIE: (*noticing the suitcase*) What's my suitcase doing here? Put it back.

HELEN: I packed it. Just in case.

CHARLIE: I'm staying here.

HELEN: You can't, Charlie. You'll be safer in a hotel.

CHARLIE: And what about you?

HELEN: What about me?

CHARLIE: This's the first place he'll look for me. Think a locked door's gonna stop him? ... Wanta know how he smokes a guy out? He roughs up the family.

HELEN: I can handle him.

CHARLIE: What makes you think that? … And let's say for the sake of argument, he doesn't kick in the door. What's to stop him from getting you after work?

HELEN: I'll tell him I don't know where you are. I'll tell him we split up.

CHARLIE: What if he doesn't believe you?

HELEN: He'll have to.

CHARLIE: What if he doesn't? … Don't expect special treatment, Helen. Don't think you have some power over him.

SAM: (*meaning CHARLIE*) I've tried talking to him, Helen. He won't listen.

HELEN: What do you plan to do, Charlie? I mean, if Bulldog's coming here at midnight …

SAM: Go on. Tell her. Tell how stupid you are.

CHARLIE: Lay off, Sam. You're starting to bug me.

HELEN: (*to SAM*) What's he gonna do?

SAM: He's gonna wait for him. He's got a gun.

HELEN: What? …

SAM: Knock some sense into him, will you? He's crazy.

HELEN: Gimme the gun, Charlie.

CHARLIE: (*to SAM*) Now see what you've done?

HELEN: Gimme the gun, I said. I mean it.

CHARLIE: Calm down, will you?

HELEN: Where is it? (*She tries to frisk him*) Hand it over, Charlie. Hand over the goddamn gun. (*She begins to pound him with her fists, but CHARLIE simply pins her arms to her sides. She breaks away*)

CHARLIE: Hear me out, will you? … As soon as that deadline's up, he thinks he's got a right to do what he likes. I'm not gonna let him hurt you, understand? If I hide out, you'll be on your own.

HELEN: You wanta get yourself killed, don't you? Is that what this is, Charlie?

CHARLIE: Don't be ridiculous.

HELEN: Well, I won't let you ... What if I went with you?

CHARLIE: And who's gonna raise the seven hundred? We both can't be holed up. You have to be free to work, and if you're free to work, he's free to get you. That's the bind.

SAM: What if she went out of town somewhere?

CHARLIE: Like where?

SAM: Moncton. (*To HELEN*) You could work there. You could live with Candy and me. Christ, between us we can raise the money in a week or two ... What do you say?

CHARLIE: It might work, Sam.

HELEN: (*to SAM*) Then why don't the four of us go together? What's it matter if Charlie hides here or down east?

SAM: Don't you see? If Bulldog tails us and finds Charlie ain't there, he just might believe you've split up.

CHARLIE: Yeah, and he might rough her up just outa spite. No, Moncton's too small, Sam.

HELEN: What about Montreal? Sam could drop me off on the way. I could work there.

SAM: (*to HELEN*) How soon can you be ready?

HELEN: I'll start packing. (*She exits into the hall and returns with a suitcase*)

CHARLIE: The thing is, Sam, you'd have to leave tonight. Next to Helen, you're at the top of the list. He'll figure for sure you know where I am.

SAM: No problem. Half our stuff's already in the truck.

HELEN: (*opens the suitcase. To* CHARLIE) Do me a favour, will you, Charlie? Get my things from the bathroom?

CHARLIE: Sure. (*He exits*)

HELEN: (*sotto voce*) Sam, I need you to do me a favour, and no questions asked ... Is Bulldog at the poolhall?

SAM: Yeah. Why?

HELEN: I want you to take me there. But I don't want Charlie to know, okay?

SAM: No way. He'd never speak to me again ... What do you want to talk to Bulldog for?

HELEN: Maybe I can get him to give Charlie another day or two. It can't hurt to try, can it?

SAM: I don't like it, Helen. I don't like it one bit.

HELEN: There's no reason Charlie has to know ... I'm thinking of him, not you, Sam ... Please. You gotta help me.

CHARLIE: (*returns, loaded down with toiletries*) Women. (*He dumps it all beside the suitcase*)

SAM: What about you, Charlie? Where you gonna go? You decided?

CHARLIE: Earl offered me a room upstairs, remember? Bulldog would never think of looking there.

SAM: Just stay away from the windows ... I'll drive you down there now, and then come back for Helen.

HELEN: Thanks, Sam.

CHARLIE: (*to* SAM) I wanta talk to Helen, okay? Give us a minute.

SAM: I'll wait outside. (*He exits*)

CHARLIE: (*to HELEN*) You're gonna need some money. (*He takes out his wallet*) Will two hundred be enough?

HELEN: That's plenty.

> *An awkward moment.*

CHARLIE: Take care, huh?

HELEN: You, too.

CHARLIE: I'll be in touch. As soon as you know where you're staying, call Earl … You sure you'll be all right?

HELEN: I'm sure … Now go on. Sam's waiting.

> *CHARLIE kisses her.*
>
> *Blackout.*

Scene Five

The poolhall. It is eleven-thirty.

EARL is sweeping the floor beside the counter. JACK THE HAT and BULLDOG are playing pool. WANDA sits at the counter, a telephone book in front of her.

WANDA: Krug, Krugel, Kruger ... Kruhl, Kruk. There he is, Earl. N. Kruk ... Can you believe it, Hat? He's in the phone book.

JACK THE HAT: Who is?

WANDA: An old trick of mine. You don't forget a name like that. " Crook " with a K.

EARL: You wanta drum up business, Wanda, use the pay phone. (*He begins to sweep the stairs*)

WANDA: Nigel. That was his name, Hat. Nigel Kruk. I always thought he made it up.

BULLDOG: Who would be dumb enough to make up a name like that? What's wrong with, say, Larry Kruk?

WANDA: Very funny ... Hey, how come you're not using earplugs, Bulldog?

BULLDOG: We ain't playing for dough, that's why. Jack lost four bills tonight, he don't wanta lose four more.

JACK THE HAT: Just shoot the ball, will you?

WANDA: (*dialing*) Was he a barrel of laughs, ole Nigel. Liked me to get dressed up in a plaid skirt and safety-pin ... (*Into the phone*) Hiya, you old horny toad. Listen, I know it's late, but ... What do you mean who's this? It's Wanda. Don't you recognize me, Nigel? ... What? Oh, I didn't know he had a brother. Well, is Nigel there? He's not, huh? ... Oh. Oh, I see. Well, thanks, Reverend. (*She hangs up*) I guess I can cross Nigel off the list. He died six weeks ago.

BULLDOG: What'd you do, give him a dose?

WANDA: For your information, I had to buy myself a plaid skirt. I always bend over backwards to give a trick a good time.

Enter AL.

EARL: (*stops sweeping the stairs*) What're you doing here, Al? Go home.

AL: What for? I wanta shoot pool.

EARL: Can't you see who's here? Go on.

BULLDOG: Don't give the man the bum's rush, Earl. He wants to be a hustler.

AL: (*to EARL*) Did Charlie come up with the dough yet?

BULLDOG: No, and don't expect him to.

AL: (*to EARL*) Thought he might be here. I got a hundred bucks for him … And I never borrowed it from a shark, Hat.

EARL: A hundred won't do much good, Al. He needs seven.

AL: (*crossing to the counter*) Yeah, well, two days just wasn't enough. Three, he mighta made it. (*He sits*)

BULLDOG: So, Al, where you think he's hiding? And don't say you don't know.

AL: You think I'd be here if I knew? … He's got a cousin in San Diego. Try there.

BULLDOG: The man's a comic, Jack.

WANDA: (*closes the phone book*) Hiya, Al. What've you been up to?

AL: Me? I just finished work … Why?

WANDA: *East of Eden*'s on the late show. Wanta go to my place and watch it on my water bed?

AL: I've seen it ten times.

WANDA: Dummy, we don't have to watch it. We can turn the set off and get seasick.

AL: Anyway, I can't. I got no dough.

WANDA: I just heard you say you had a hundred.

AL: That's for Charlie.

WANDA: He ain't gonna need it now. You heard Earl.

AL: No, I wanta hang around here … Can you change a quarter, Earl? (*EARL does*)

WANDA: Jeez, forget I offered … What a lotta deadbeats.

AL: (*playing the pinball machine*) Besides, why should I pay for it? I got a girl who's dying for it, just dying for it.

JACK THE HAT: Maybe she'd like a rest, Al.

WANDA: Yeah. Give the girl a break.

AL: Anyone needs a rest, it's me. Ever seen how a cat sharpens its claws on wood? She does the same on my back.

BULLDOG: That's another crock.

AL: Oh, yeah? Well, I've got the scars to prove it.

BULLDOG: The way this man brags, Jack, he must have more stitches than a football. I don't think he's even got a girl, do you? He ever bring her around, Earl?

AL: She don't like poolhalls.

BULLDOG: Bet he sits at home, slicking down his hair with Brylcreem and playing "Love Me Tender." (*To JACK THE HAT*) The man's locked up in the fifties.

Enter SAM and HELEN.

WANDA: Well, well, look who just walked in ... What're you doing down here, Helen, slumming?

JACK THE HAT: Who's the dish? You know her?

BULLDOG: Yeah, I know her. It's his old lady.

JACK THE HAT: Sam's?

BULLDOG: No. Charlie's. (*He returns to the game*)

HELEN: (*crossing to the table*) Hello, Bulldog.

BULLDOG: You got a helluva nerve, you know, coming in here ... What do you want?

HELEN: Can I see you outside?

BULLDOG: Your shot, Jack. (*To SAM*) Get her outa here before she gets hurt.

EARL: Now wait just a minute ...

SAM: Come on, Helen. I told you it was a bad idea. Let's go. (*He goes to take her arm, but she shakes him off*)

HELEN: No. I wanta talk to him.

BULLDOG: If your husband sent you here to ask for favours, don't bother. He's got twenty minutes.

EARL: Give the lady a break, Bulldog. Have some respect.

BULLDOG: Stop sticking your nose in, Earl. This don't concern you ... (*To HELEN*) Okay, you wanta talk to me, talk to me. But make it quick.

HELEN: Does it have to be a circus? Couldn't we talk in private?

BULLDOG: I'm busy. Talk to me here or forget it.

HELEN: All right ... Look, Charlie's come up with almost all the money he owes you. He can raise the rest if you just give him a day or two ... Will you do that?

BULLDOG: If that's all you wanted, you're wasting your breath. He's already had two days. (*He turns back to the table*) And if you figured you could get what you want just by twitching your tail, you figured wrong.

HELEN: I don't understand, Bulldog. What do you gain by hurting him? What's he ever done to you?

BULLDOG: (*To HELEN*) I'll even the score.

HELEN: Haven't you already done that?

BULLDOG: No. The satisfaction was all yours ... Now beat it.

HELEN: (*stands her ground*) You know, the day Charlie told me how you made your living, I don't think I believed it. That's how naïve I was.

BULLDOG: I only hurt chiselers.

HELEN: He's not a chiseler, he's a hustler. And the people he scams think they're hustling him.

WANDA: Oh, yeah? Well, what about Greg?

HELEN: That was different, Wanda. For Chrissake, you know the fix Charlie's in.

WANDA: Too bad. Look at the fix I'm in.

HELEN: None of this would be happening, if you hadn't hustled him. He woulda taken the bet to the track.

SAM: He owes three Gs, Wanda, because of you. Let's not forget that.

HELEN: He only scammed Greg 'cause he was desperate. He doesn't want his legs broken. Can you blame him?

BULLDOG: (*to JACK THE HAT*) Would you send your woman here to plead for you? A man who'd do that deserves what he gets. (*To HELEN*) How can you respect a man like that?

HELEN: He doesn't know I'm here. It was my idea, not his.

BULLDOG: Yeah, sure.

HELEN: (*beat*) I'm asking you again, Bulldog. Will you just give him one more day? … I'm not asking for him. I'm asking as a favour to me.

BULLDOG: (*tosses his cue on the table*) Why should I let him off the hook for you? Think you're worth three G's? I wouldn'ta looked at you twice if you hadn't been his wife.

HELEN: So I've been told.

BULLDOG: (*crosses to her*) Yeah, and every night you scratched on my door, I'd think to myself, This is for you, Evans. Who's the better man now? … Hell, I coulda made *you* pay three G's you wanted it so bad.

> *HELEN slaps his face hard.*

BULLDOG: Why, you little … !

> *He pulls back his arm to strike her, but SAM rushes at him and deflects the blow. BULLDOG twists SAM's arm behind his back and pushes him face forward onto the table. (NOTE: From the moment this happens, a chorus of protests erupts, EARL rushing out from behind the counter and WANDA and AL leaping off their stools).*

AL: Dammit, Bulldog. You'll hurt him.

EARL: This's gone too far. I'm gonna put a stop to it right now. (*To HELEN*) You never shoulda come here. (*He starts for the front door*)

SAM: (*still pinned to the table*) Earl! Don't! Wait!

> *EARL exits.*

WANDA: Let him up, Bulldog. You'll break his arm.

AL: The stupid bastard don't know his own strength.

BULLDOG: (*steps away from SAM*) What'd you call me?

AL: Who? Me? … Nothing.

BULLDOG: (*grabs a ball from the table*) See this, cabdriver? It'll crack your head open like an egg. You're not outa here in ten seconds, I'll do it ... Two, four, six, eight ...

> *AL dashes for the front door and exits.*

WANDA: Do something, Jack. The guy's gone berserk.

BULLDOG: The Hat knows when to keep his nose out, don't you, Jack?

JACK THE HAT: It's your call, Bulldog.

SAM: (*sotto voce*) We gotta get outa here, Helen. Earl's gone upstairs ... Let's go.

BULLDOG: (*to HELEN*) Hey, I'm not gonna hurt you ... You want that extra day? All you gotta do is walk over here and ask.

WANDA: I wouldn't trust him, if I was you.

BULLDOG: (*to HELEN*) You wanta buy him more time? Or don't you?

SAM: He's just toying with you, Helen. Let's go.

> *HELEN hesitates. Then she crosses the floor and stands in front of BULLDOG.*

HELEN: All right, I'm here.

BULLDOG: Get down on your knees. Go on ... (*He puts his hands on her shoulders and presses her down*) Now beg me. I wanta see how far he'll let you go.

> *Just then, CHARLIE bursts in, followed by EARL.*

BULLDOG: (*to HELEN*) Go on. Beg me, and maybe I'll give him another day.

CHARLIE: Don't beg him, Helen. For Chrissake, don't beg him ... Get up. (*He helps her up*)

BULLDOG: Where the hell was he hiding, Earl? Upstairs? ... What gives?

CHARLIE: (*to SAM*) What'd you bring her here for? Don't you know better than that? Goddamn you, Sam.

HELEN: It's not his fault.

BULLDOG: One thing I can say for her: she's got guts. She wasn't hiding under some bed, with the blinds drawn.

> *CHARLIE draws his gun, aims it at BULLDOG, and cocks the hammer.*

CHARLIE: One more word, Bulldog, and so help me ...

EARL: Oh, Jesus ...

HELEN: Don't be stupid, Charlie. Put down the gun.

WANDA: You'd be doing us all a favour, Charlie, but it's not worth it. They'd throw the book at you.

BULLDOG: Better keep on that side of the table, flat ass ...

WANDA: Or what? Lay a hand on me, and I swear to God I'll sign a statement.

BULLDOG: You're gonna threaten me once too often, Wanda.

WANDA: When he pimped for me, he'd drive by and pick up his dough ... then knock me around. I had more bruises than Al has stitches.

BULLDOG: You had a big mouth, even then.

WANDA: He always thought he was God's gift to women. Well, lemme set you straight, Bulldog, for old time's sake. Charlie's a better lay than you. Take it from me.

BULLDOG: You're a liar.

WANDA: Am I?

BULLDOG: Why don't you ask his wife? She might have a different opinion.

HELEN: Even better, Bulldog, why don't you ask me which of you I'd die for? Maybe that's more to the point. (*She looks over at CHARLIE*)

Pause. CHARLIE slowly lowers the gun.

EARL: Jesus H. Christ.

CHARLIE: You know, Bulldog, a guy just like you once took Earl's game away from him. But you know what? Earl still knew he was the best.

WANDA: (*beat*) Want that extra day, Charlie? I can make Bulldog give it to you. Just say the word.

CHARLIE: Thanks, Wanda, but I won't be needing it. (*He crosses to the counter and hands EARL the gun*) Here, Earl. Get rid of this, will you?

EARL: Will do.

HELEN: Charlie … ?

CHARLIE: It's okay. I know what I'm doing.

BULLDOG: Time's almost up, Evans,

CHARLIE: Don't worry, Bulldog, you're gonna get your three G's.

BULLDOG: How?

CHARLIE: How? I'm gonna whip your ass, that's how. You think you can do that to her? Pick up your cue.

SAM: (*to CHARLIE*) Now you're talking.

EARL: Too bad Al wasn't here to see this.

BULLDOG: (*chalking his cue*) The man's finally agreed to play me. How 'bout that? … So, Evans, what happened to your principles?

CHARLIE: (*to HELEN*) Do me a favour, will you? Go home … I wanta do this on my own.

HELEN: You sure, Charlie?

CHARLIE: I'm sure … I'll see you later.

WANDA: (*to HELEN*) What do you say we share a cab?

> *HELEN and WANDA start for the front door. HELEN stops.*

HELEN: Charlie.

CHARLIE: (*powdering his hands*) Yeah?

HELEN: I won't wait up. But wake me.

CHARLIE: I may be late.

HELEN: Wake me, anyway.

CHARLIE: Okay, I will.

WANDA: Crack him out, Charlie. For me.

> *HELEN and WANDA exit.*

JACK THE HAT: Hey, Charlie, you want my cue? Take it.

CHARLIE: Thanks for the offer, Jack, but I'll get my own. (*He picks a cue from the rack, then crosses to the corner pocket. Takes out his wallet*) Maybe you think you've won something already, Bulldog, by getting me to play. And maybe you have. But you know what I'm gonna do? I'm gonna take that smile off your face and beat you with it.

SAM: Atta boy, Charlie.

BULLDOG: Nothing like confidence, is there? … How much we playing for?

CHARLIE: (*to SAM*) Your call.

SAM: Play him for a thousand, Charlie. A thousand, to start.

BULLDOG: A thousand?

CHARLIE: Yeah? You chicken? (*He sticks the money in the corner pocket*)

BULLDOG: Don't make me laugh. (*He counts his money and stuffs it in the pocket*)

EARL: This kind of action draws crowds.

JACK THE HAT: I'd like to bet on this one, Bulldog. You interested?

BULLDOG: In what?

JACK THE HAT: I'd like to put five hundred on Charlie. To win.

BULLDOG: You gotta be kidding.

JACK THE HAT: I have a hunch he'll take you.

BULLDOG: You think so? ... You're covered. (*He and JACK THE HAT toss five hundred in the pocket. To CHARLIE*) Jack always liked the long shots.

CHARLIE: Only at the track, Bulldog. Call it. (*He flips a dime on the table*)

BULLDOG: Heads.

CHARLIE: You break.

> *BULLDOG stuffs cotton batting in his ears. Then he breaks ... CHARLIE carefully lines up a shot ... SAM turns and walks towards the front door. He looks back as CHARLIE shoots, then turns and exits.*
>
> *As the ball rolls slowly across the table—*
>
> *Blackout.*